# SOUTH CAROLINA'S
# MATILDA EVANS

# SOUTH CAROLINA'S MATILDA EVANS

*A Medical Pioneer*

Walter B. Curry Jr., EdD, Anusha Ghosh
and Beverly Aiken Muhammad

*Foreword by Bobby Donaldson, PhD*

THE
History
PRESS

Published by The History Press
An imprint of Arcadia Publishing
Charleston, SC
www.historypress.com

First published 2025

Manufactured in the United States

ISBN 9781467159081

Library of Congress Control Number: 2024951903

*Notice*: The information in this book is true and complete to the best of our
knowledge. It is offered without guarantee beyond the stated research on
the part of the authors or The History Press. The authors and The History
Press disclaim all liability in connection with the use of this book.

*The cyclic nature of time always gives us the opportunity to remember our loved ones from times gone by. And by remembering them we are given another chance to honor them. I, along with my cousin, Dr Walter B. Curry, and my dear friend, one whom I consider as family, Anusha Ghosh, dedicate this great work, first of all to the legacy of my grandmother, Dr. Matilda A. Evans, for she was the epitome of dedication.*

*Dedication is defined as having a commitment so strong to something that it sets you above and apart. Dedication renders the person who is committed to their purpose an unparallel upward mobility which is rewarded by advancement and achievement. My grandmother's work clearly defined dedication to such an extent that we remain inspired today by her extraordinary achievements.*

*Often in the glory of such achievement there are those who were there, actively supporting and benefiting from such a cause. Considering such, I wish to also dedicate this great work to the children of Dr. Evans, who might never be known otherwise. These are my uncles and aunts who kept her alive as a family. They are my mother, Mattie Olga Evans Aiken, Uncle John B. Evans, (who managed our family restaurant, The College Inn on Harden Street, right across from Benedict College), Aunt Gretchen Matilda Evans Jenkins, Aunt Jessie Trottie Hill (who lived for many years in the historical home of Dr. Evans at 2027 Taylor Street, Columbia, South Carolina), Aunt Myrtle Evans, Uncle Sidney Trottie, and Uncle Edward Evans.*

*And to the grandchildren of Dr. Evans: myself, my brother, James Evans Aiken, my first cousin, Mary Agnes Evans Smalls, and my sister Olga Mauvene Aiken Swanson, who requested her body be donated to the University of Texas in the name of her grandmother Dr. Evans upon her passing recently. And to the great-grandchildren of Dr. Evans: Kariem Shabazz Ali Hammonds, Keshia Gretchen Aiken, Gerald Smalls, Tariq Majied Akbar Ali, Kellie Smalls, Nadia J. Muhammad and Brad Evans Aiken.*

*We, the immediate and extended family, are extremely grateful to countless others, both Black and White, who for over one hundred years, have contributed to the great works of Dr. Matilda A. Evans. Especially to Martha Schofield, the great Quaker educator of Aiken, South Carolina, The University of South*

Carolina and the pioneers of the historic Waverly Community of Columbia, South Carolina.
Let us never forget that "Success is not final; failure is not fatal: it is the courage to continue that counts." As such, though we are her immediate family, in all actuality her legacy belongs to each one of us. As such, this work is also dedicated to each and every one of you. May God bless us all in her name.
Very lovingly submitted, Beverly Aiken-Muhammad

———◆———

Thank you to my parents, who traveled across the world to provide me and my siblings better life, health, and education. Thank you to Dr. Bobby Donaldson and Dr. Burke Dial for guiding me during my research on Dr. Matilda Evans, a pillar in the Waverly Community and a role model for future healthcare workers. Lastly, thank you to Dr. Curry and Mrs. Aiken-Muhammad for the opportunity to contribute to this monumental book. I hope to do my part in relaying the timeless legacy of Dr. Evans and the critical subject of civil rights in healthcare toward my fellow peers in medical school.
Cordially, Anusha Ghosh

———◆———

Thank you to my cousin Beverly Aiken-Muhammad for entrusting me in the research and curation of her legendary grandmother Dr. Matilda Evans. Thank you to Anusha Ghosh for trusting me to assist with your research on Dr. Evans. Special thanks to Dr. Bobby Donaldson for continued preservation of Columbia African American history promoting Dr. Evans's legacy. I dedicate this book to my lovely wife, Takiyah S. Curry, for your dedication and exemplary service in the field of health care and mentorship to African American women pursuing health careers in nursing; my cousins, Tay Moore, MD, and Curry Cheek, MD; and my sons, Braxton Lee Roosevelt Curry and Braylon Simon Curry. This work is also dedicated to you, the reader. May God bless you and we pray that you will be inspired by the legacy of Dr. Evans.
Cordially, Walter B. Curry Jr., EdD

# ODE TO DR. MATILDA EVANS

WRITTEN BY JENNIFER BARTELL BOYKIN
POET LAUREATE OF THE CITY OF COLUMBIA, SOUTH CAROLINA

*You were at a funeral when you fell ill.*
*They took you back to your house on Taylor Street*
*where you took your last breath.*
*But before that last breath was all the other breaths*
*you had in that house. The patients whose hearts*
*you checked, the white women who came to you for*
*gynecology services, the children with tuberculosis.*
*The days you sat by the window,*
*with your pen writing for the Negro Health Journal,*
*planning ways black people could get free,*
*quality healthcare in the middle of separate but unequal.*
*Your foster children all around, reminding you of your purpose.*

*Matilda means mighty in battle*
*and you kept the faith,*
*fought the good fight.*

*You weren't in for the money.*
*You weren't in for the praise,*
*though you received plenty.*
*You were in it for the people.*
*You were in it for the healing.*

*The health of the people is wealth*
*when you have your health*
*you have everything,*
*and you gave folks your everything*
*even Though the smog of capitalism and*
*racism made it hard to breathe.*

*Your house on Taylor Street is still here.*
*Your fight for free healthcare is still here.*
*Your love for the health of Black folks*
*is still here.*

*Germs still don't abide*
*by the color line.*
*Breath still our survival,*
*breath still how we spread*
*viruses and diseases.*

*You were a young woman when you came*
*to Columbia. Your eyes trained on this vision.*
*Black people have the right to quality healthcare.*
*You opened hospitals and free clinics,*
*trained nurse and doctors, Black and white,*
*always coming back to the house on Taylor Street.*
*Taking your rest after a full day of work, your*
*breath slowing into sleep.*

# CONTENTS

# Contents

# FOREWORD

*Her life is truly a beacon for all young people today who find it difficult to maneuver through life's twists and turns. Her life is also a constant reminder to those of us who are older to stay the course and not seek the easy or most convenient way out.*
*—Burnett W. Gallman Jr., MD*

*It is not easy to write about Dr. Evans and her work without indulging in superlatives—superlatives which would be heartily endorsed by many of both races.*
*—A.B. Caldwell*

*All the circumstances considered, the Negro race has made and through its leaders continues to make history more creditable. A deplorable situation, however, arises out of neglect to record and preserve the worthwhile achievements we are constantly bringing to pass. In consequence, it becomes a duty—a duty mingled with pleasure—to give the widest publicity to the splendid achievements and inspirational examples of a pronounced success so outstanding as Dr. Evans's, whose whole career is a legacy invaluable to rightfully ambitious youths of both sexes.*
*—Reverend John R. Wilson*

As a professor of African American history at the University of South Carolina, I am honored to pen a foreword to a timely volume that seeks to "record and preserve the worthwhile achievements" of one of South Carolina's most distinguished citizens—Dr. Matilda Arabella Evans. The authors are to be commended for crafting a compelling and informative tribute to a gifted scholar, a staunch activist and an enterprising medical professional who was hailed as "South Carolina's brainiest Negro" and as the "dean of Negro physicians in South Carolina."

One of South Carolina's first African American women to earn a medical degree, Dr. Matilda A. Evans journeyed from the rural fields of Aiken County to the heart of downtown Columbia. Her story is more than a narrative of personal achievement—it is a story of resilience and dedication to public health, education and the welfare of African Americans during a time when the barriers of segregation and racial prejudice were seemingly insurmountable.

As this narrative documents, Dr. Evans was a person with immense gifts and talents shaped by a supportive family and dedicated educators and mentors. With deft diplomacy, she defied custom and convention. With resolve, and certainly moments of doubt and setbacks, she shattered stereotypes and successfully carved out a unique space of her own.

This book reminds us of her origins and the paths she pursued from the prayerful hopes of Reconstruction and the New Negro Movement to the deferred dreams of Jim Crow redemption and the Great Depression. We learn about her network of friends, the medical professionals she trained and the patients she treated. And we learn much more about her family—the kinfolk who reared her and the expanded circle of children and grandchildren that she molded and inspired.

Like my mother's family, Dr. Evans's roots run deep in Aiken County, and like my grandmother Ruby, Dr. Evans graduated from the Schofield Normal and Industrial School, where she was mentored by the school's founder, Martha Schofield. In 1916, after Schofield's passing, Dr. Evans published a book titled *Martha Schofield, Pioneer Negro Educator: Historical and Philosophical Review of the Reconstruction Period of South Carolina*. In some respects, Evans's historical investigation provides a revisionist assessment of Reconstruction, especially as it highlights the repeated "reign of terror" African Americans witnessed and experienced in the decades following Emancipation. But the work is also an appeal for Black ingenuity, independence and governance. On the eve of World War I, and in anticipation of the platforms of Marcus Garvey and Malcolm X, Dr. Evans remained convinced that the forces of White supremacy would never enable progress among her people. She remarked:

> *By every test or qualification and efficiency, the Negro in government, in the science of war, in the art of agriculture, in manufacturing, invention,*

*medicine, law, and literature, is well prepared to assume the government of his race in a territory of his own. This insures him the same protection from the persecution and injustices of the stronger race that enabled the latter to succeed so famously when they too, in the course of human events, found it necessary to dissolve the political bonds that united them to a dominant authority that gave them no justice.*

This emphatic cry of "no justice" came from a female African American doctor in South Carolina in the early twentieth century. Who was Dr. Matilda A. Evans? What shaped her worldview? And how did her medical practice and social activism affect her community? Fortunately, these questions are answered in the archival and genealogical revelations provided by the authors in this volume.

As you turn the pages of this publication, you will learn of Evans's humble beginnings, her tenacious pursuit of education and medical training, the establishment of her practice in Columbia, the creation of free clinics for young people and struggling citizens, the publication of historical volumes and the *Negro Health Journal* of South Carolina, her leadership in the Palmetto Medical Association, the Negro State Fair Association and her pioneering role in establishing hospitals, nursing facilities, and other business ventures.

As you read this biography, you will develop a deeper appreciation for a captivating personality who attracted the attention of Dr. W.E.B. Du Bois, who included her achievements in the NAACP's *Crisis* magazine, and Tuskegee Institute president Booker T. Washington, who wrote about Dr. Evans in his book *The Story of the Negro*. You will witness the journey of a woman described by writer Charles Stewart as someone that others "gazed upon as a wonder of the age."

In the spring of 1905, Stewart, a writer for the *Afro-American* newspaper, traveled across South Carolina meeting with African American leaders. He later chronicled his encounters in his "Midnight's Musing" column. In the article titled "Greatness of the American Negro not Generally Known to Mankind," Stewart recalled a meeting with an enterprising and accomplished young physician in Columbia, South Carolina. He observed:

*I want to introduce you this week to Dr. Matilda Evans, who has dyed with the same black goods that is mixed in me. She is a lily black and would not be taken for a white woman on the dark of the moon. She is possessed of one of the greatest intellects and hearts to be found in any human being. I admire her because she brought something into existence, and she is giving her life to bless mankind. I am sending her picture and will take time to tell you about her so as to inspire other girls of my race.*

*She is recognized as one of the ablest physicians and surgeons in the whole state of South Carolina, and you will understand that I did not say colored.....No, she is a physician and a good one at that. It would pay you to see what a woman is doing for her race.*

Four years later, in the summer of 1909, Dr. Matilda Evans riveted residents of Wilmington, Delaware, when she spoke to an interracial audience of over two hundred people attending a fundraiser sponsored by the Philanthropic Committee of the Wilmington Monthly Meeting of Friends. After Evans delivered a speech titled "A Colored Woman's Work in Establishing a Hospital" and recalled her journey from rural Aiken County, one audience member observed: "I believe she is a woman so sincere in her purpose to do for her brothers and sisters with so much grit, energy, dignity, and ability that she will succeed."

As you turn the pages of this book, you will learn more about Dr. Evans' "grit, energy, dignity, and ability," and you will see why audiences across the country were captivated by her speeches and presentations. You will gain a greater understanding of why Dr. Evans was revered as a "pioneer Negro Physician," "one of the ablest physicians and surgeons in the whole state of South Carolina," an "unusually intelligent Negro," "one of the foremost colored women in the country" "an apostle of sanitation and better living conditions."

This biography, and the broader archival evidence, demonstrate clearly that Dr. Evans was, in the words of Reverend John R. Wilson, "a pronounced success." She was indeed a skilled and highly acclaimed physician and pioneering public health advocate whose work and activism demonstrated that health equity was essential in the quest for civil and human rights.

As you delve into this book, may you find not only a reflection of the past but also a guide for the present and future reminder that the fight for equality, justice and wellness is a continuous journey, one that Dr. Matilda A. Evans's enduring example compels us to join.

Bobby Donaldson, PhD

# ACKNOWLEDGEMENTS

*T*he authors wish to express their gratitude to those who have played a significant role in the research and publication of this book, including Bobby Donaldson, PhD, Associate Professor of History and Director of the Center for Civil Rights History and Research at the University of South Carolina-Columbia; Bill Barley, photographer and owner of Bill Barley & Associates Inc.; Cynthia Hardy, President of the Aiken-Barnwell Genealogical Society and Director of the Wagener Museum; Debbie Livingston Bass, a descendant of John W. and Sarah Kitchings Brodie; Smyrna Missionary Baptist Church in Springfield, South Carolina; the Martha Schofield Alumni and Legacy Organization; the family of Dr. Matilda Evans; Chad Rhoad, Senior Acquisitions Editor at The History Press; and Stacy Lipscomb, niece of Jessie L. Trottie Hill, who is also the niece of Dr. Matilda Evans.

# INTRODUCTION

*Walter B. Curry Jr., EdD*

My maternal ancestral roots run through Aiken County, South Carolina, in the rolling hills and pastures on the outskirts of Salley, South Carolina. The rolling hills and pastures that dominate the small community of Salley have an extraordinarily rich history. The area's history includes stories of African American people and experiences documented through ancestry and local history.

I connected with a fellow family historian whose ancestors were slaves on the Brodie plantation in Kitchings Mill, located between Salley and Aiken, South Carolina. She revealed that her ancestor married into the Evans family. Throughout our discourse on our ancestries, she shared information about a prominent African American woman of the Evans family. She shared that the woman named Dr. Matilda Abrabella Evans was an African American woman of historical significance and recommended that I learn more about her. I first discovered that Matilda was South Carolina's first native-born African American woman medical doctor, and she grew up in eastern Aiken County, South Carolina. Upon this discovery, I began to learn more about Matilda's education as a scholar student at Schofield Normal & Industrial Institute under the mentorship of the legendary Quaker, abolitionist and education pioneer Martha Schofield. I also learned about Matilda's fascinating journey to become a medical doctor, her lifework in providing quality health care services among African

Americans in South Carolina, her work in addressing health disparities among African Americans during racial segregation in South Carolina, and her work in expanding healthcare access for African American and White families in South Carolina.

I located a copy of the book *The Southern Workman*, published by the Hampton Institute Press in 1906. The chapter "The Story of a Negro Child's Resolve" is a compelling biographical account about Matilda. While reading the chapter, I discovered an ancestral connection to Matilda and her family. Matilda's maternal great-grandmother, Phyliss Corley, is my fourth-great-grandmother! Phyliss married John Corley, and together they had a son named Harry Corley, who is Matilda's maternal grandfather. Harry and my third great-grandmother Lavinia Corley Thompson are half siblings; both share the same mother. Harry married Edith Willis, and together they had three children: George Corley, Frances Corley and Harriet Corley. Harriet married Anderson Evans and gave birth to Matilda and her siblings Andy and Ora.

One day I visited my maternal family church, Smyrna Missionary Baptist Church, located near Springfield, South Carolina. Smyrna is one of the oldest African American Baptist churches in eastern Aiken County and its vicinity, founded in 1873 during the Reconstruction era. The church has a rich history that includes formerly enslaved people, successful farmers, entrepreneurs, musicians, ministers, military veterans and educators. Smyrna is the resting place of my ancestor Lavinia Corley Thompson, South Carolina's only African American woman to receive a state Confederate pension for military service.

In touring Smyrna's cemetery, I stumbled across a marble headstone of Matilda's father, Anderson, and his second wife, Mary. Then, a few yards from Anderson and Mary's headstone, I stumbled across the marble headstones of Matilda's grandmother Edith and her uncle George. The discovery of Matilda's family grave markers at Smyrna was truly an epiphany moment! I was further intrigued by this discovery, read Smyrna's church history and discovered that Matilda's mother, Harriet, was one of the founders of the church.

One day I was surfing the South Carolina Legislature Online website researching pending legislation focusing on education and historical preservation. I looked up pending legislation from my resident state senator, Mia McCleod, and found that she sponsored legislation honoring Matilda's legacy. I immediately reached out to her office to introduce myself. Senator McCleod's assistant told me that they wanted to connect with Matilda's descendants, and I mentioned that I would assist. I then connected with Matilda's granddaughter Beverly Aiken-Muhammad, and she reached out to me. Since our connection, we have collaborated in speaking engagements, interviews and research on Matilda's life. Beverly published a book, *A Case for Separation: Inspired by Dr. Matilda Evans, MD.* The book is a critical and reflective analysis of African American life and experiences through Matilda's eyes through the African American radical tradition.

Matilda's inspirational life is curated immensely throughout South Carolina and beyond. Since her death in 1935, Matilda has become a legend, an inspiration of pride, a shero and a trailblazer in the annals of African American history, women history and medicine. While there is a breadth of research, there has never been a book published on Matilda's background and her illustrious journey into medical practice. I, along with Beverly, agreed that Matilda's story should be published to present her groundbreaking contributions in healthcare among African Americans visible for reading and further study. Finally, we concurred that Matilda's contributions to the advancement of African American people in South Carolina is worthy of recognition with lessons in empathy, leadership, educational pursuit, career advancement, addressing health inequities, medicine breakthroughs, religious faith, collaborative initiatives and community service.

This book presents a revolutionary account of Matilda's life, delving into her extraordinary journey. It seeks to engage readers through Matilda's story of resilience and meaningful existence, honoring her as a cherished historical figure and heroine of South Carolina.

# I
# THE ANCESTRAL JOURNEY OF MATILDA EVANS

*From Enslavement to Liberation and Beyond*

*We are the accumulation of the dreams of generations.*
—*Stephen Robert Kuta*

## EDITH WILLIS CORLEY

Edith, the daughter of Henry and Julia Willis of Chester, Pennsylvania, was born free in 1812.[1] During the antebellum period, Chester was a prosperous manufacturing community with industries such as shipbuilding, textiles, locomotive and machinery.[2] The city was a major stop of the Underground Railroad for runaway slaves escaping to the North for freedom.[3]

In 1850, tensions between free and slave states evolved into sectional conflicts over the issue of slavery and its expansion. Congress passed several bills known as the Compromise of 1850.[4] The compromise temporarily diffused tensions between free and slave states in the years leading up to the Civil War. Designed by Senator Henry Clay of Kentucky and Senator Stephen A. Douglas of Illinois, with the support of President Millard Filmore, the compromise centered on how to manage slavery in the recent acquired territories from the Mexican American War. The compromise bills included the Fugitive Slave Act, which required all escaped slaves, upon capture, to be returned to the enslaver, and that local officials and citizens of free states had to cooperate.[5]

The Fugitive Slave Act attempted to deter the substantial number of runaway slaves from border states. The border state of Maryland had 279 runaway slaves.[6] As a result of the Fugitive Slave Act, slavecatchers had free rein to operate in free states to catch runaway slaves. Many slavecatchers saw an opportunity to capture African Americans in free states through kidnapping.[7] Kidnappers operated in northern urban cities of free states, where they used deceptive tools and strategies to lure their victims.

In his biography *Twelve Years a Slave*, Solomon Northup, a freeborn African American from New York, recounted his experience being drugged and kidnapped into slavery in Washington, D.C.:

*Two or three colored servants were moving through it, one of whom, a woman, gave me two glasses of water. It afforded momentary relief, but by the time I had reached my room again, the same burning desire of drink, the same tormenting thirst, had again returned. It was even more torturing than before, as was also the wild pain in my head, if such a thing could be. I was in sore distress—in most excruciating agony! I seemed to stand on the brink of madness! The memory of that night of horrible suffering will follow me to the grave. The pain in my head had subsided in a measure, but I was very faint and weak. I was sitting upon a low bench, made of rough boards, and without coat or hat. I was hand cuffed. Around my ankles also were a pair of heavy fetters. One end of a chain was fastened to a large ring in the floor, the other to the fetters on my ankles. I tried in vain to stand upon my feet. Waking from such a painful trance, it was some time before I could collect my thoughts. Where was I? What was the meaning of these chains? Where were Brown and Hamilton? What had I done to deserve imprisonment in such a dungeon? I could not comprehend. There was a blank of some indefinite period, preceding my awakening in that lonely place, the events of which the utmost stretch of memory was unable to recall. I listened intently for some sign or sound of life, but nothing broke the oppressive silence, save the clinking of my chains, whenever I chanced to move. I spoke aloud, but the sound of my voice startled me. I felt of my pockets, as far as the fetters would allow—far enough, indeed, to ascertain that I had not only been robbed of liberty, but that my money and free papers were also gone! Then did the idea begin to break upon my mind, at first dim and confused, that I had been kidnapped. But that I thought was incredible. There must have been some misapprehension—some unfortunate mistake. It could not be that a free citizen of New York, who had wronged no man, nor violated any law, should be dealt with thus inhumanly.*[8]

The presence of kidnappers alerted the abolitionists and antislavery organizations, who warned African Americans in free states to be cautious. Advertisement campaigns about kidnappers lurking in the urban cities of free states were prevalent.[9] The kidnappers' actions were deeply controversial and had significant implications during the time when the abolitionist movement was gaining momentum in free states such as Pennsylvania, where Edith and her family lived.

Like Solomon Northup, Edith lived free and happy until she was kidnapped by slavecatchers while socializing with her friends.[10] The slavecatchers spirited off with Edith to Charleston, South Carolina, where she was sold in the slave market and taken to the Orangeburg District, South Carolina.[11] The district's economy was heavily dependent on slavery and cotton yet prospered. Large plantations using slave labor were established in Orangeburg District during the nineteenth century, and the district became a major producer of cotton.[12] Orangeburg's geographical diversity was unique compared to other districts in South Carolina during the antebellum period. According to historian William Hine:

*In 1790 the district had 12,412 white people, 5,931 slaves, and 170 free people of color. By 1860 the white population had declined to 8,108 while the number of slaves nearly tripled to 16,583, and the free black population was 205. In 1860 there were 1,069 slaveowners in the district, thirty-three of which held over one hundred slaves. Orangeburg's farms and plantations produced sixteen thousand bales of cotton in 1860, as well as sizable quantities of corn, wheat, oats, rice, sweet potatoes, and wool. In addition, the district contained two carriage factories and several lumber mills, especially along the timber-rich Edisto River. Orangeburg District was also a prominent link in the state's transportation system. The Congaree, Santee, and Edisto Rivers were important navigable waterways, while the State Road between Charleston and Columbia ran through St. Matthews, Cameron, and Holly Hill. In 1833 part of the South Carolina Canal and Rail Road Company's railroad crossed the southern part of Orangeburg. With the construction of a branch line to Columbia, the world's first railroad junction was created at Branchville in 1840.*[13]

Like any other human phenomenon, slavery has multiple facets and can be viewed from various perspectives. While the Slave Code defined slavery uniformly across the South, there were differences in regulations imposed on slaveholders and slaves depending on the state. Despite these variations, slavery was a consistent legal institution throughout southern states. Conversely, the actual conditions of slavery varied not only across various parts of the country but also from one plantation to another.[14] Each plantation operated as a distinct community, with life shaped by the collective actions of those involved. The treatment of slaves by slaveholders was influenced, to some extent, by the laws and customs of the surrounding area.

# The Corley Family

Edith was not so unfortunate as she might have been, for her enslavers were people of religious sensibilities who were considerate of their slaves and treated her with kindness.[15] On arriving at womanhood, Edith married Harry Corley, the son of John and Phyliss Corley, who were enslaved by Joshua Corley.[16] Joshua owned a large estate near the town of Windsor, South Carolina, located in the Barnwell District, South Carolina. He was a farmer who owned thousand of acres of land and served as the justice of the quorum. According to the 1850 Slave Census, Joshua held twenty-two slaves in bondage.[17]

In 1855, Phyliss's daughter Lavinia, who was nicknamed "Sina," was the primary subject of a legal dispute between Joshua and his son-in-law Samuel Webb. The legal dispute led to a petition filed by Samuel. A written summary of the petition mentioned the following:

*Samuel Webb seeks to recover two slaves from his father-in-law, Joshua Corley. Webb represents that Joshua gave him three slaves in 1843. The slaves remained in his possession until the summer of the present year when Joshua took possession of Sina and her daughter Jane. When Webb attempted to regain possession of the two slaves, Joshua and his son Thornton gave him various excuses. Thornton claimed that Joshua had deeded the two slaves to him and to Sampson Corley. He asserted, however, that he was prepared to release the two slaves if Webb executed a document wherein he agreed to place the slaves in trust for the benefit of his wife and children and to deliver the slaves to Thornton and Sampson whenever they deemed it fit. Webb refused to sign. Webb avows that Sina is very valuable to him and his family. Her "constitution temper and qualities are good" and "attachments have grown up" between her family and his. He claims to have been offered a price for Sina beyond her market value and to have refused the offer because Sina is of "peculiar value" to him. Webb therefore seeks an order compelling Joshua and Thornton Corley to deliver Sina and Jane to him and to account for the value of Sina's hires since she has been in their possession.*[18]

Lavinia's granddaughter Nettie Thompson Johnson recorded an oral account that Lavinia shared with her grandchildren about the time she was persecuted for her defiance when Joshua initially sold her to a slaveholder in Tallahassee, Florida:

*Viney Corley Thompson is the wife of Reverend Logan Thompson. Mary Woodward Evans is the wife of Daniel Evans. Both were born to a slave mother from Africa, who was brought here on a boat. The morning Viney (as she was called) and Mary were going to be sold in Tallahassee, Florida the two girls talked it over and each said they were going to listen real good to hear and see where they were being sold to and to whom. But we do know that Viney was sold for $100.00. Grandma Viney later told her story to some of her grandchildren (Nettie Thompson Johnson, Uncle Oscar's daughter) Grandma Viney said "I must have been the pretty thing that day because I bought in that much money." She told the slave auctioneer "You might as well sell me over because I ain't a go'." At the time, her dress was white. Her master beat her all the way home 'till her dress was so bloody that you couldn't see the white on it. Later in life Viney and Mary found each other. Sometimes later Viney's granddaughter, Nettie Johnson would be in church and see this lady at Smyrna Baptist Church in Salley, S.C. and thought it was grandma Viney. It was Viney's sister Mary W. Evans. Both were very strong women and lived to be very old grandmothers.*[19]

Harry and Edith were both dark in complexion.[20] Together, they had three children: Frances Corley, George Corley and Harriet Corley Evans. Although South Carolina's Negro Act of 1740 made it illegal for enslaved people of color to write, Edith made sure that her children received a proper education.[21] She taught her children the best she could herself. Edith sent her children to school and paid their teacher by washing blankets at night for local Whites long after everyone had gone to sleep.[22] Edith's daughter Harriet Corley, besides her formal education, was taught sewing and became a skilled seamstress.[23] Having a beautiful voice, Harriet learned how to sing and became a soloist.[24] She was often called to entertain the local White community at festive occasions.[25]

# THE BRODIE FAMILY AND THE KITCHINGS MILL COMMUNITY

Before the Civil War, a large planter and slaveowner named John Wardlaw Brodie Sr. purchased Edith and her children.[26] During the 1820s, John and his wife, Sarah Kitchings Brodie, migrated from Charleston, South Carolina, to Kitchings Mill, located in Orangeburg District, near the South Edisto River.[27] Kitchings Mill was founded by two brothers who migrated from Charleston. Kitchings Mill was a unique community known for its beautiful timber, and the abundance of trees attracted migrants who sought to earn a living in the lumber industry. John and his father were in the lumber business.[28] They cut the timber and floated the lumber in rafts down the nearby South Edisto River to the Lowcountry markets where it would be sawed and shipped.[29] Kitchings Mill was one of fourteen mills that operated in the western part of Orangeburg District.[30] The mills were of immense importance and produced wheat flour, cornmeal and cut lumber.[31] The mill also served as a gathering place for the local people.[32] Some mills were located near stores that included a post office for people to receive mail. Many individuals and families made a good living from a well-run mill.[33]

Life in Kitchings Mill was full of recreation activities. According to historian Micheal Kitchings Roof,

*Women occupied themselves with household chores and rearing children much of the time, however, there was always time for pleasure. They enjoyed horseback riding, quilting, gardening, and working for the church. Dancing was prevalent in the community; however, the church was not pleased with this form of pleasure. Men enjoyed fox hunting, log rolling, fish fries, and farming. The fish fries were held especially when they came together to clear land for a fellow farmer. When a farmer had hard times, because of sickness, the farmers throughout the community would gather to assist this ill farmer. Their efforts included working his crops until he recuperated.*[34]

The Brodie family owned a plantation named Oak Grove near Kitchings Mill.[35] The plantation house was two stories, built out of cypress wood and originally had four large columns on the front of the house.[36] The kitchen area was at the back of the house, joined by a porch or walkway.[37] Several agricultural crops, including upland rice, were planted and harvested at Oak Grove.[38] According to the 1860 Slave Census, the Brodie family owned twenty-two slaves.[39]

In 1860, Orangeburg's farms and plantations yielded a total of sixteen thousand bales of cotton, along with significant amounts of corn, wheat, oats, rice, sweet potatoes and wool.[40] According to the 1850 Agricultural Census, on the plantations owned by Josuha Corley and John Wardlaw Brodie Sr., corn was their primary cash commodity.[41] The census reported that Joshua produced one thousand bushels and John produced five hundred bushels of Indian corn.[42]

The Brodies and other White families attended Tabernacle Baptist Church near Kitchings Mill.[43] The church was founded in 1830 and became the predominant religious center of Kitchings Mill during the antebellum period.[44] In the early years of Tabernacle, the membership consisted of Whites and enslaved African Americans. Racially segregated sitting was allowed. Married ceremonies among slaves were conducted by a White minister of the church.

Historian Micheal Roof Kitchings described the significance and influence of Tabernacle Baptist Church in Kitchings Mill history:

*The setting of Kitchings Mill Community was one of serenity and concern. The church in the area was Dean Swamp Baptist Church, the mother church of Tabernacle Baptist Church. Because of the immobility of this time in history, Tabernacle created a more centrally located place of worship for the community. For those who love the Lord, Tabernacle Baptist Church created a meeting place to meet the demands of the growth of the community. It was once said that members often walked to church for their day of worship. Sunday was the day for Tabernacle Baptist Church and worship. On a Saturday night, many residents would kill a hen or get a ham from the smoke house to prepare for the Sunday dinner. This allowed them to arrive at church on time and concentrate; instead of worry, "what's to be for dinner." After the Worship Service, dinner was prepared already, and the families merely sat down to the meal. The only thing left undone was brewing the coffee. It has been said that the community members and the church members were one in the same. These folks were concerned with each other and enjoyed fruitful periods of fellowship.*[45]

# THE CIVIL WAR

On December 20, 1860, delegates across South Carolina met in Charleston to propose that South Carolina secede from the Union. Dissatisfied with the election of Abraham Lincoln to the presidency, the delegates believed President Lincoln would impose high tariffs on cotton that would adversely affect South Carolina's economy, which depended on slavery. The convening body of delegates, known as the South Carolina Secession Convention, issued an Ordinance of Succession, formally announcing South Carolina's withdrawal from the Union. The ordinance read:

> *To Dissolve the Union between the State of South Carolina and other States united with her under the compact entitled "The Constitution of the United States of America." We, the People of the State of South Carolina, in Convention assembled, do declare and ordain, and it is hereby declared and ordained, That the Ordinance adopted by us in Convention, on the twenty-third day of May, in the year of our Lord one thousand seven hundred and eighty-eight, whereby the Constitution of the United States of America was ratified, and also, all Acts and parts of Acts of the General Assembly of this State, ratifying amendments of the said Constitution, are hereby repealed; and that the union now subsisting between South Carolina and other States, under the name of "The United States of America," is hereby dissolved.*[46]

South Carolina, along with seven other states, established the Confederate States of America in February 1861. On the early morning of April 12, 1861, Confederate guns opened fire on Fort Sumter near Charleston, South Carolina. This action led to the beginning of the bloodiest war in American history, known as the Civil War. Districts across South Carolina, including Orangeburg, overwhelmingly supported the Confederacy.[47] Orangeburg District was a major stronghold that supported nullification, a legal theory that a state has a right to invalidate any federal laws it deems unconstitutional, which was one of the core beliefs of the Confederacy.[48]

In the early years of the Civil War, South Carolina began to mobilize for war. Districts across South Carolina began to recruit volunteers to serve as soldiers and in nonmilitary roles. Most of the Confederate military force in South Carolina were poor White men, enslaved laborers and free African American men who were drafted, but there were some slaveowners. John Wardlaw Brodie Sr. volunteered to support the military effort.[49] On January 12, 1862, John died of a heart attack while working for the Confederacy processing saltpeter for making gunpowder.[50] On Wednesday, January 15, 1862, the *Charleston Daily Courier* announced his obituary:

*Obituary DIED At his residence Oak Grove Orangeburg District S C on under the 12th inst. - Mr. JOHN WARDLAW BRODIE in the 66th year of his age. Mr. Brodie was a native of Charleston—Early in life he emigrated to Orangeburg District where amid many provisions and embarrassments he reared a very numerous family to position of usefulness and respectability wrought of his own fortune by diligence and enterprise, and earned for himself a spotless reputation. Within the last twenty years he formed a connection in business in Charleston and became more widely and favorably known in the active walks of mercantile life of his native city where his sterling integrity manly dealing transparent honesty, lofty sense of honor and modest self-respect secured for him the confidence and esteem of his fellow citizens. Strict and even rigid in his exactions of duty from himself yet full of clemency forbearance and charity he ever strove to forget overlook and hide the faults and infirmities of others.*

*Ardent and loyal in his devotion to his native State he ever exhibited a lively interest in her honor and welfare He was firm faithful and confiding in his friendships; sincere tender and affectionate in his attachments and in his general intercourse with the world kind and courteous doing honor unto all men His beneficence was bountiful indeed—he seemed to feel that he was but the trustee and almoner of those goods wherewith it had pleased God to endow him. His house was the abode of hospitality; the friendless, the indigent, the afflicted, and the bereaved always found in him ready succor and sympathy. Humility was the crowning grace of his character in deriving himself and seeking to do God's will he found his own inward peace, freedom, and happiness. So passed the honorable useful and well-spent life of this good man.*

*The brief and simple inscription which by his own dying request will mark the repository of his earthly remains is enough. The grave of the just man is a hallowed spot the cherished memory of his virtues is his epitaph their record in Heaven is his reward. He rests in peace: he falls asleep in Christ—The graves of all his saints he blessed, when in the grave he lay; and rising thence, their hopes He raised to everlasting day.*[51]

Before his death, John prepared a will in Charleston on May 31, 1861.[52] In the will, he left Oak Grove and the slaves, including Edith and her three children, to his wife, Sarah.[53] After John's death, life on Oak Grove was interrupted by the looming presence of Union soldiers who were looting plantations, burning homes and destroying property throughout South Carolina, including nearby Barnwell District. The Barnwell District town of Williston was burned and pillaged by Union soldiers according to Mary Phillips Harvey, who published her account in 1925:

*My home was in ruins—a mass of brick and ashes. The flower yard trampled by the feet of many horses, and pieces of my piano scattered around. Some kind-hearted soldiers, (for some kind) saved it from the flames, only to be broken in pieces by others. Some even cut the wires out with an axe and gave them to some poor people who lived near us, and they made knitting needles of it.*[54]

After the destruction of Williston, Union soldiers marched toward the Dean Swamp community, located a few miles from Kitchings Mill. The soldiers ransacked the property of Allan Porter, who owned a large tract of land in Dean Swamp. In 1923, in an interview with a reporter, Emma Porter Brodie, the daughter of Allan Porter, recalled her eyewitness account of the destruction of her father's property by the soldiers:

*Early Sunday morning they began to arrive. There only three in the first party. The weather was terribly cold, and the negroes had already made a fire for us. When men walked in, we piled on more wood and invited them to come up to the fire. They seemed to be perfect gentlemen. However, in a few minutes the mob swarmed in like bees. They were all over the premises in almost no time. They literally ransacked the whole place. A negro man who came with them, stepped to me and said: "You are the finest looking young lady I've seen since I left the North." My goodness! I was scared to get out of the house rest of that day and night. That party finally went away and another came. One of these men was so drunk that he rode his horse right on into the kitchen porch. And so it went on all through that terrible never-to-be forgotten day and night! Sorrow and destruction above us, a Mr. Williamson was quite ill in bed with measles. He was tied to a horse and led away. His family never heard of him again.*[55]

Fortunately, when the troops came through Kitchings Mill, the destruction was milder than expected. Oak Grove was one of the few remaining plantation homes in Kitchings Mill that was spared. In his research, historian Paul Roof Kitchings shared an account about a group of Union soldiers showing sympathy when they stopped at one home in Kitchings Mill:

*One story is told that the troops stopped at one home and discovered the horses. They took them all, except an old lame mule. The troops did show some sympathy. When one of the lieutenants decided to take a quilt on which a small child was resting, his superior told him to leave it there. He stated that he had a child at home approximately the same age.*

The devastating years of the Civil War had a profound effect on South Carolina and the rest of the South, resulting in the death or disability of many Southern men. The war officially ended on April 9, 1865, when Confederate General Robert E. Lee surrendered to Union General Ulysses S. Grant at Appomattox Court House. Two months later, on June 19, 1865, Union soldiers, under the command of Major General Gordon Granger, arrived in Galveston, Texas, and declared the end of the war and the freedom of the enslaved. The official abolition of slavery in the United States took place on December 6, 1865, with the ratification of the Thirteenth Amendment. This marked a new reality for formerly enslaved individuals, who became known as freedmen.[56]

# THE EARLY YEARS OF THE RECONSTRUCTION ERA

Edith had reached the age of fifty-three when slavery was officially abolished. Her family, like many others who were once enslaved, had to adjust to their newfound freedom. They faced the challenges of meeting their basic needs independently, obtaining education and adapting to life as freed individuals. The difficult circumstances of Freedmen prompted Congress to pass the Freedmen's Bureau Act of 1865. This legislation established the Freedmen's Bureau, which aimed to assist and safeguard Freedmen in the Southern states.[57] The bureau was authorized to provide aid to both Freedmen and White refugees, offering services such as medical care, education and the redistribution of abandoned lands to former slaves.[58] The Freedmen's Bureau represented a significant democratic initiative during the Reconstruction era (1865–77). This period marked a crucial time in American history as the nation sought to reconcile its divisions and integrate formerly enslaved people into society. The bureau played a vital role in supporting formerly enslaved people as they navigated the challenges of transitioning to freedom and rebuilding their lives.

The crisis of formerly enslaved people was so visible in the Orangeburg District that Union Captain Charles Soule wrote a letter to the head of the Freedmen Bureau, General Oliver Otis Howard, advising him of the formerly enslaved people's new condition:

*To the Freed People of Orangeburg District. You have heard many stories about your condition as freedmen. You do not know what to believe: you are talking too much; waiting too much; asking for too much. If you can find out the truth about this matter, you will settle down quietly to your work. Listen, then, and try to understand just how you are situated. You are now free, but you must know that the only difference you can feel yet, between slavery and freedom, is that neither you nor your children can be bought or sold. You may have a harder time this year than you have ever had before; it will be the price you pay for your freedom. You will have to work hard, and get very little to eat, and very few clothes to wear. If you get through this year alive and well, you should be thankful. Do not expect to save up anything, or to have much corn or provisions ahead at the end of the year. The plantation you live on is not yours, nor the houses, nor the cattle, mules, and horses; the seed you planted with was not yours, and the ploughs and hoes do not belong to you. Now you must get something to eat and something to wear, and houses to live in. How can you get these things? By hard work and nothing else, and it will be a good thing for you if you get them until next year, for yourselves and for your families. You must remember that your children, your old people, and the cripples, belong to you to support now, and all that is given to them is so much pay to you for your work. There are different kinds of work. One man is a doctor, another is a minister, another a soldier. One black man may be a field hand, one a blacksmith, one a carpenter, and still another a house servant. Every man has his own place, his own trade that he was brought up to, and he must stick to it. The house servants must not want to go into the field, nor the field hands into the house. If a man works, no matter in what business, he is doing well. The only shame is to be idle and lazy. Do not think of leaving the plantation where you belong. If you try to go to Charleston, or any other city, you will find no work to do, and nothing to eat. You will starve or fall sick and die. Stay where you are, in your own homes, even if you are suffering.*[59]

Despite achieving some victories, the Freedmen's Bureau faced challenges as many formerly enslaved people continued to experience systemic racism and economic hardship. In 1865, South Carolina implemented a constitution that introduced minor democratic reforms, such as electing governors and granting veto power, while eliminating property requirements for officeholders.[60] However, the constitution also disenfranchised qualified African Americans and enforced restrictive Black Codes that limited formerly enslaved people's freedom of movement.[61]

Many of the formerly enslaved people who lived in Kitchings Mill after the war had virtually nothing. The Kitchings Mill area referred to as the "The Skillet" was so named for the challenges that formerly enslaved people faced in making a living there. In his book *A History of the Brodie Family 1754–1993*, Al Brodie detailed the history of the Skillet:

*After The Civil War, there were many freed black slaves who had nothing—particularly land or homes. A Mr. Livingston, who at that time was the Sheriff of the Orangeburg District, was a large landowner in the area, and he gave 1,000 acres of land to the blacks in that area. The recipients of this land really had it tough, having to clear the land, make it formidable, and build homes. Knowing that it was going to be rough going, at one of their initial meetings, one of the blacks said, "Well, we will have to lick the skillet clean"—meaning they couldn't leave a crumb in the pot. Hence the name of the black area of Kitchings Mill became known as the "The Skillet," and as time passed, the name became inclusive in the entire area.*[62]

# THE EVANS FAMILY

While some formerly enslaved people settled in the Skillet, Edith and her children continued to live on Oak Grove for a few years. While living on Oak Grove, Harriet met and married a formerly enslaved person named Anderson Evans, who was of mixed heritage.[63] The newly married couple moved to Charleston.[64] Charleston served as the military headquarters for the occupying Union forces during Reconstruction (1865–77).[65] Freedmen migrated to Charleston in large numbers in search for better economic opportunities. During their stay, Anderson and Harriet welcomed the birth of their oldest child, Matilda Arabella Evans, who was born on May 13, 1869; Ora Evans; and their only son, Andy Evans.[66] The family's stay in Charleston was short, and they returned to Kitchings Mill, settling into farming life.[67]

Upon the Evans family's return to Kitchings Mill, the community was a part of the newly formed Aiken County, founded on March 10, 1871.[68] African American men Prince Rivers, Charles D. Haynes, Samuel J. Lee, William B. Jones and others founded Aiken County, which is the only county founded by African Americans in South Carolina, according to records from the Reconstruction era.[69] The county was named after William Aiken, the first president of the South Carolina Railroad and Canal Company.[70] Aiken County was formed from parts of Barnwell, Lexington, Orangeburg and Edgefield Counties.[71] The Orangeburg County section taken to form Aiken County was Kitchings Mill, where the Evans family lived.

On Thursday, April 27, 1871, the *Intelligencer* reported details of the official legislative act that established Aiken County and the commissioners who marked the county boundaries:

*Approved March 10, 1871. An act to establish a new judicial and election county from portions of the counties of Barnwell, Edgefield, Lexington, and Orangeburg, to be known as Aiken County. Section 1. Be it enacted by the Senate and House of Representatives of the State of South Carolina, now met and sitting in General Assembly, and by the authority of the same. That a new judicial and election County, with its seat of justice located at the town of Aiken, which County shall be known as Aiken County, shall be formed, and is hereby authorized to be formed, from portions of the present Counties of Barnwell, Edgefield, Lexington and Orangeburg, with the metes and bounds hereinafter described, to wit: commencing at the mouth of Fox's Creek, in Edgefield County, where it empties into Savannah*

*River, thence in a straight line to where the South branch of Chinquapin Falls Creek (a tributary of the North Edisto River) intersects the Edgefield and Lexington line; thence down said creeks to where it empties into the North fork of the Edisto River, and down the said north fork to where the dividing line between Lexington and Orangeburg Counties (running from Big Beaver Creek to the North fork of the Edisto) touches said river; thence in a straight line to the head of Tinker's Creek, in Barnwell County; thence down said creek to where it empties into the Upper Three Runs, and down said Runs Creek to where it empties into the Savannah River; thence up the Savannah River to the initial point at the mouth of Fox's Creek. Sec. 2. That Frank Arnim, M.F. Maloney, P.R. Rivers, J.L. Jamison, E. Ferguson, J.N. Hayne, E.J.C. Wood, P.R. Rockwell, J.A. Greene, W.H. Reedish and B. Byas be, and are hereby appointed Commissioners to run out and properly mark and define the said boundary lines, with the assistance of two competent surveyors to be selected by them. Sec. 3. That S.J. Lee, Frank Arnim, P.R. Rivers, C.D. Hayne. John Wooley, E.J. Wood, J. Hayne, Levi Chavis, W.H. Reedish and J.H. Cornish be, and are hereby, appointed Commissioners to provide suitable.*[72]

The Evans family was unique compared to the other African American families in Kitchings Mill. Anderson established himself as leader among African Americans in the community.[73] Anderson was respected and beloved for his charitable giving to the poor and less fortunate. As a mother, Harriet held lofty expectations for her children and promoted the importance of education. The family briefly attended Tabernacle Baptist Church, the church of their former enslavers.[74] Racially segregated seating was disallowed, and African American and White members sat together in the church.

## The Founding of Smyrna Missionary Baptist Church

During the Reconstruction era, Baptist congregations serving African Americans formed throughout rural South Carolina. African American members of White Baptist churches began to form their own churches. In 1873, Smyrna Missionary Baptist Church was founded to serve African American families who lived in Kitchings Mill and surrounding areas.[75]

The founding members of Smyrna, including Harriet, were given letters of dismissal from Tabernacle.[76] The site to build Smyrna was selected about two miles from the present site.[77] A White minister named Reverend J.E. Zeigler served as moderator, and his son Felder served as clerk.[78] The land for the church was donated by Tabernacle and cleared by local African Americans to build a brush arbor to host church services.[79] Baptism services were held in nearby pond.[80]

During the early years at Smyrna, the atmosphere of church time was always lively and enthusiastic. Despite the small size of the wooden church building and the congregation, which consisted of sharecroppers and neighbors, the worshippers experienced a powerful connection with God.[81] The preachers delivered powerful sermons that led to the salvation of many souls. People of all backgrounds and ages, both young and old, enthusiastically sang and shouted during services at Smyrna Missionary Baptist Church.[82] The annual revival meetings held in June were highly anticipated and considered just as important as traditional holidays. On Saturdays, the congregation would prepare for the big meeting on Sunday by engaging in various tasks. Men and older boys woke up early to butcher meat, while women cooked it in large pots and pans over open fires. Children chased down chickens to prepare for the meal. As the day ended, everyone cleaned up using water from the pumps or Shaw's Creek. The women took the time to groom themselves, iron their clothes and ensure everything was prepared for a full day of worship at church.

Smyrna was filled with worshippers from various churches who gathered for revival meetings. Despite the lack of a breeze, the preachers delivered powerful sermons under the shade trees, accompanied by electrifying singing. The congregation eagerly awaited the closing "Amen" after the intense worship. Women and older girls worked hard to prepare a delicious meal—including greens, cornbread, corn, okra, peas, squash, hog meat, chicken, cakes, pies and more—for the attendees. The tables were adorned with starched white tablecloths, and nearby, large watermelons awaited to be enjoyed. As the congregation sat at the long wooden tables, they swatted away gnats and flies while relishing the feast and reconnecting with old friends and family. The children hurriedly finished their meals to have time to play before the next church service.

The Evans family, along with Edith and George, were members of Smyrna. The church membership included formerly enslaved people, ministers, tradesmen, businesspeople and military veterans, including Harriet's aunt Lavinia Corley Thompson, who served as enslaved cook in the Confederate army.[83] Lavinia is the only African American woman in South Carolina to receive a state Confederate pension. Edith briefly served a stint as the church mother due to her age and wisdom. Lavinia husband, the Reverend Logan L. Thompson, served as an ordained minister.

## Racial Violence in Aiken County

The Reconstruction era in Aiken County saw the formation of racial violence and electoral corruption. The majority population of African Americans in the town of Hamburg made the town a Republican stronghold. Because Hamburg wielded so much political power in Aiken County, the town became the bane of White Democrats, who were envious of African Americans holding political office.[84] Tensions flared between African American Republicans and White Democrats during the election of 1876, in which Aiken County witnessed bloody race riots in Hamburg on July 8, 1876.

Historian Wayne O'Bryant described the events of the Hamburg Massacre:

*As the nation's centennial was approaching, former Confederate soldiers from Edgefield County were devising schemes that they hoped would allow them to wrestle control of the state from "Negro Rule." The initial target was Hamburg. On July 4, 1876, two white men, Tommy Butler and Henry Getzen, attempted to drive their horse drawn buggy thru the formation of the Black militia who were drilling in the center of Market Street in Hamburg. The altercation resulted in words being exchanged but the militia eventually opened ranks and let them through. Butler's father, Robert Butler, hired former Confederate General Mathew Butler (no relation) as his lawyer to swear out a complaint against the militia. When Gen. Butler demanded that they surrender their guns, they refused, and all hell broke loose. A mob of several hundred White men had gathered in Hamburg throughout the day. Two dozen Black militia men had taken cover in their armory when the firing began. The mob even employed a cannon in the attack. By the end of the night, two Black men and one White man had been killed and a few dozen Black men were taken captive. What happened next would go down in history as "The*

*Hamburg Massacre." The White mob began to take unarmed Black men out of the ring of men who encircled them, and one by one began to execute them. After killing four men, some in the mob called for the killing to stop. The remaining prisoners were released and told to run. As they fled, a final volley of shots was fired into the fleeing crowd wounding some, one later died bring the final death toll to eight (one White and seven Black). After the Hamburg Massacre, White rifle clubs united under the banner of "The Red Shirts" and unleashed a reign of terror across the State. They attacked Black citizens throughout the months leading up to the November elections. On Election Day, armed White men manned the polls to keep Black men from voting and in some counties ballot boxes were stuffed resulting in thousands more votes than there were voters. The steal would prove to be successful. Yet, in the fog of the contested SC election, a deal was being struck in the presidential election. South Carolina promised to give their electoral votes to Rutherford B. Hayes, giving him the Presidency, if he would in turn remove Federal Troops from the South, thus ending Reconstruction. Hayes was losing the popular vote in South Carolina, so he made the deal. South Carolina delivered the winning electoral votes, and Hayes kept his end of the bargain. With Federal troops withdrawn, the era of Reconstruction was over, those who lost power after the war were back in power, and Americans of African descent were stripped of their Civil Rights including their precious right to vote. The death of Reconstruction ushered in the Jim Crow Era. Within one short decade, the flame of the American Ideal, that all men were created equal, had been lit and extinguished.*[85]

A few months after the Hamburg Massacre, a racial riot broke out around the town of Ellenton, a former community that was located on the border between Aiken and Barnwell Counties. The riot started when rumors circulated in the community that a group of African Americans assaulted an elderly White woman. On Wednesday, October 4, 1876, the *Newberry Weekly Herald* reported:

*The Ellenton riot may be summed up as follows, as taken from the letter of Gen. Hagood to the Journal of Commerce. Gen. H., upon the information of the disturbance, was authorized by Judge Wiggin of the Second Circuit of South Carolina, to collect as strong a force as possible and act as the posse comitatus, under the orders of: Sheriff Jas. Patterson, to suppress the riot and arrest the ringleaders. It was not an unauthorized mob. Four hundred and seventy-five citizens of the county, mounted and armed, responded to the call, among whom was the Barnwell Colored Democratic Club. Mr. Patterson, while riding in advance, was shot from ambush and badly wounded. He is now doing well. When Gen. H. arrived at the scene. he found that the citizens from the vicinity had suppressed the riot, for the present at least, and that the negroes had fled to the swamps. Seeing no necessity for keeping the men from their homes they were dismissed, and warrants were issued against the ringleaders, with orders to arrest and take them to Barnwell jail for trial. The casualties were two whites killed, one wounded seriously, three slightly. The number of negroes killed, including the fighting in Aiken County, is about thirty.*[86]

During the time of the Ellenton riot, an incident occurred at Smyrna Missionary Baptist Church where members of the Ku Klux Klan tried to apprehend a young man accused of a crime.[87] The Klan shouted obscenities at the congregation, demanding the young man come out, prompting the women to gather the children and usher them inside the church. Reverend Logan L. Thompson and the men of the congregation confronted the Klan, forming a protective circle around the young boy. Two Klansmen aimed a shotgun at the young man's face, but a carload of Klansmen intervened, instructing them to leave the young man alone and head to Ellenton. The Klansmen eventually left the revival meeting after striking the young man with a shotgun. A woman from the church applied homemade salves and bandaged his wound with a clean rag. The congregation prayed for the young man's safety, and their bravery in defending him inspired new members to join the church.

## MATILDA EVANS'S FAMILY LIFE IN THE POST-RECONSTRUCTION ERA

The Reconstruction period concluded in 1877. During that year, Harriet fell ill and passed away.[88] Prior to her passing, she provided her brother George with detailed guidelines on how to raise Matilda. With only $160 to leave behind, she instructed her brother to use the money for Matilda's education. Harriet's final words were, "If the child is neglected, she will never amount to anything and may grow up to be a bad woman, but if she is educated, she will be good and help to educate other children."[89]

Following Harriet's passing, Anderson wedded a woman named Mary, and they resided in Rocky Grove township of Aiken County, where Salley, South Carolina, was established on December 20, 1887.[90] The town was named after Dempsey H. Salley, a state legislator who was instrumental in its incorporation and bringing the railroad to the region.[91] Situated on a one-thousand-acre plantation owned by Salley, the town thrived with amenities like naval store manufacturers, a hotel, a school and churches, attracting families of both African American and White descent.[92] Eli Salley, an African American, was employed by Salley's railroad company, the Blackville, Alston and Newberry Railroad Company, while Cora Salley became the town's first postmaster.[93]

After her mother's death, Matilda lived with her grandmother Edith and her uncle George in Rocky Springs township, located in mid-eastern Aiken County, South Carolina.[94] Although Matilda's father was still alive after the death of her mother, Edith took on the responsibility of raising Matilda.[95] She also established herself as a community nurse focused on healing the sick.[96] In the post-Reconstruction era, grandmothers played a significant role in their communities. They reared children, educated them in their own homes, delivered babies and provided indigenous medicines for both African American and White families. Without economic and political resources, grandmothers like Edith continued to promote the importance of kinship among African Americans.

The system of sharecropping was firmly established as the accepted and preferred form of agricultural labor on cotton farms and plantations in South Carolina during the Reconstruction and post-Reconstruction eras. Sharecropping was a type of farming in which families rented land from a landowner in return for a portion of the crop to be given to the landowner at the end of each year. Sharecropping life was challenging work, full of uncertainties. They had to work constantly to ensure their survival. The inconvenient truth about sharecropping was that the landowner had the most power. Sharecroppers were under constant pressure to perform well for the landowner or face expulsion from the property.

A viable alternative for many African American sharecroppers was landownership. Landownership was a goal for Edith and her family to escape the trappings of sharecropping and tenant farming. Through hard work and sacrifice, in 1880, Edith and George accumulated money and purchased two hundred acres of land in Rocky Springs, paying only $600.[97] On the land, family raised livestock and crops and used machinery to till the land. Edith and George wanted to ensure the economic security of the family.

George was an herbalist who gathered herbs and provided medicinal care to the poor in the community.[98] George and other herbalists were in demand and offered herbs to cure patients of common cold, yellow fever and other illnesses. Herbal medicine was quite common throughout South Carolina in the bygone days and was widely used by African Americans, Native Americans and Whites alike. During the 1890s, the *Aiken Standard* vigorously promoted herbal medicines. On November 8, 1899, the *Aiken Standard* interviewed John Corley, an African American herbalist who lived in Aiken and was a hoodoo doctor:

*Seventy-Six Years Old-John Corley, an old colored resident of the city, seventy-six years of age, is a remarkably well-preserved man. He is native of this county, having been born and raised in Tabernacle township. Uncle John or Dr. John, take your choice, as he claims to be a hoodoo doctor says he enjoys fine health now, although in his younger days he suffered much with backache and other troubles. While experimenting with herbs and roots for something to cure backache and neuralgia he discovered a remedy that not only cured him, but he says it will cure any case of rheumatism even after other doctors have failed. Dr. John claims that he can now go out in the woods and cut and split 200 rails a day. Says he has been married three times and is the father of about sixteen children, and six years ago his children, grandchildren and great-grandchildren numbered seventy-six. He does not know the number to date, but at the rate of increase they were accumulating we should judge the correct figure wouldn't fall short of one hundred. Dr. John was at the train with his basket of hoodoo medicines on his arm waiting on the arrival of a patient from Montmorenci. The Doctor has only been living the city since January.[99]*

Observing her uncle, Matilda caught on to ideas through imaginative play by "playing doctor, steeping leaves to make medicines, rolling bits of clay into pills, and practicing on the chickens that she caught running around the ground."[100] The imaginative play underscored Matilda's upbringing in her family that uniquely prepared her to become a medical doctor. Matilda's parents, grandmother and uncle ensured that she had a solid foundation for her future.

# MATILDA EVANS'S EDUCATIONAL JOURNEY

## *Shaped by Historical Events and Aspirations for Personal Success*

Throughout history, the African American community has consistently seen education as a pathway to bettering their social standing. This unwavering belief in education was demonstrated through the establishment of schools by prominent Black leaders, the formation of literary societies and the encouragement of others to make use of these educational institutions. While some philanthropic White groups, like the Quakers, did establish schools to provide basic education for African American individuals, the African Methodist Episcopal Church also played a significant role in founding schools. Additionally, the African American intelligentsia united to create literary societies that not only offered libraries but also served as platforms for the exchange of ideas on various topics of interest.

## PENNSYLVANIA

Pennsylvania, the native state of Matilda's grandmother Edith Willis Corley, provided educational opportunities for African Americans in the early nineteenth century, although racial discrimination was prevalent. The Pennsylvania Abolition Act of 1780 aimed to gradually end slavery and remove discriminatory laws, but it failed to ensure equality for Black citizens.[101] The prevailing belief in Black inferiority and the fear of racial mixing resulted in segregation and discrimination across social, political and economic aspects of life. However, African American individuals actively worked to improve their situation by forming self-help organizations, with education being seen as a crucial solution to the challenges faced by the community. Education opportunities were provided for poor children in Pennsylvania regardless of racial background. The Pennsylvania Constitution of 1790 mandated that each county should establish schools for impoverished children, with the state covering teacher salaries.[102] The Pennsylvania Abolition Society was successful in petitioning for public funding for the education of African Americans in 1820 and lobbied for the first tax-supported public school for African Americans in 1822 in Philadelphia.[103] The society received minimal resistance from White citizens if the schools were segregated.

Public schools established during the antebellum period were deemed insufficient, with separate schools for African Americans showing signs of improvement but still facing discouraging conditions.[104] The disproportionate allocation of school funds resulted in classes being held in poorly ventilated and ill-equipped buildings, with a lack of well-trained African American instructors and competent White teachers avoiding these positions due to low wages and social ostracism.[105] This led to a high turnover in the teaching staff, with a basic curriculum in African American schools reflecting the prevailing belief in the mental inferiority of Blacks, despite efforts by individuals like Anthony Benezet to challenge this prejudice.[106] Despite their shortcomings, these schools played a crucial role in teaching many African Americans to read and write, as well as inspiring some to pursue further education.

# THE STONO REBELLION

In contrast, during the time Edith began her life of forced servitude in South Carolina as a slave, the state enacted strict laws to govern slaves because of the aftermath of the Stono Rebellion. The Stono Rebellion was one of the first slave revolts in South Carolina and was the largest in British North American history. On February 3, 2000, *The State* newspaper reported the events of the rebellion:

*On Sept. 9, 1739, a large group of South Carolina slaves, Angolans mostly, gathered on the banks of the Stono River southwest of Charleston. The group's intentions were simple and deadly. They planned to steal as many weapons as they could, kill as many whites as they could and flee to Spanish-controlled Florida and freedom. The rebellion echoed similar uprisings earlier that year in the Caribbean islands of Jamaica, Antigua and St. Christopher's. The Stono Rebellion, as it came to be known, was not the first or last slave revolt in South Carolina. But it was the largest slave revolt in British North America. When the uprising ended a week later, 75 people, white and black, were dead. The slaves who gathered at the Stono River bridge, about 20 miles southwest of Charleston, broke into Hutchenson's Store and stole arms and ammunition. They cut off the heads of the storekeeper and the clerk and displayed them on the front steps. The group then moved south on the main road, looting homes and farms and killing all the whites they could find. Other slaves joined the rebellion as it moved south, drawn by word of mouth and drum calls. South Carolina Lt. Gov. William Bull, for whom Columbia's Bull Street is named, came upon the group of rampaging slaves, which now numbered about 100. He wheeled his horse, outran his pursuers and spread the alarm.*

*Over the next week, every white male was armed and went in pursuit of the slaves. Indians also were hired to track down and kill the renegade slaves. Forty to sixty blacks were killed outright. Some of slaves were decapitated by militiamen, their heads displayed on mileposts marking the revolt's progress south. One of the leaders hid [in] Lowcountry swamps for three years before he was betrayed and hanged.*[107]

The Stono Rebellion, a failed but violent endeavor, involved around one hundred slaves who aimed to escape to St. Augustine in Spanish-controlled Florida and secure their freedom. This uprising stands as South Carolina's deadliest and most significant slave insurrection. The uprising led to attempts to restrict the actions of enslaved individuals and emancipated African Americans.

# LEGAL RESTRICTIONS IN TEACHING SLAVES AND THE MUDSILL THEORY

A year after the rebellion, the South Carolina General Assembly passed the Negro Act of 1740.[108] The legislation established the legal framework for a developed colonial community that relied on enslaved labor. It formalized the exclusion of slaves from the protections of English common law, rendering them legally insignificant. Slaves were prohibited from giving testimony under oath, with the accounts of White individuals taking precedence. The killing of a slave by a White individual was downgraded to a minor offense, punishable by a monetary penalty. Curiously, a slave could physically defend their master's life against a White person but was prohibited from doing the same to protect their own life. The penalties for slave offenses were heightened, with death sentences being authorized for planning rebellion (or escaping), setting fires or teaching other slaves about poisonous plants. Any White individual, not just slaveholders, was granted the power to apprehend and penalize Black individuals who violated the law.

In addition, the Negro Act of 1740 included a provision that prohibited the teaching of writing to slaves.[109] South Carolina feared if slaves were taught to write or slaves were employed as scribes in any manner of writing, it could entice slaves to rebel. Therefore, the act decreed that if anyone was found instructing slaves to write or using them for writing tasks, they were fined one hundred for each offense. Although reading was not forbidden under the act, the teaching of reading to slaves was culturally feared among slaveowners. The fear stemmed from the belief that if slaves could read and write directions, they could strategically plan their escape and insurrections.

Ninety-four years after the passage of the Negro Act of 1740, in 1835, the South Carolina General Assembly passed an act that prevented the teaching of slaves or free African Americans and abolished African American schools. The act read:

*This law was: An act to amend the law relating to Slaves and Free persons of Color. Be it enacted by the Honorable, the Senate and House of Representatives now met and sitting in General Assembly, and by the authority of the same. If any person shall hereafter teach any slave to read or write, or cause or procure any slave to read or write, such person if a free white person upon conviction thereof shall for each and every offense against this act be fined.*[110]

Slave education was strictly prohibited, while the education of free persons of color was closely monitored, with a White person required to supervise if the teacher was a person of color.

The belief that slaves were intellectually inferior and lacked skills led to legal restrictions on their access to literacy education. Slaveowners, such as Senator James Henry Hammond of South Carolina, viewed slaves as belonging to a lower class and were destined to serve the upper classes and society. In a speech to his colleagues on March 4, 1858, Senator Hammond presented the Mudsill Theory:

> *In all social systems there must be a class to do the menial duties, to perform the drudgery of life. That is, a class requiring but a low order of intellect and but little skill. Its requisites are vigor, docility, fidelity. Such a class you must have, or you would not have that other class which leads progress, civilization, and refinement. It constitutes the very mudsill of society and of political government; and you might as well attempt to build a house in the air, as to build either the one or the other, except on this mudsill. Fortunately for the South, she found a race adapted to that purpose to her hand. A race inferior to her own, but eminently qualified in temper, in vigor, in docility, in capacity to stand the climate, to answer all her purposes. We use them for our purpose and call them slaves. We found them slaves by the common "consent of mankind," which, according to Cicero, "lex naturae est." The highest proof of what is Nature's law. We are old-fashioned at the South yet; slave is a word discarded now by "ears polite;" I will not characterize that class at the North by that term; but you have it; it is there; it is everywhere; it is eternal.*[111]

Senator Hammond contended that every society needed a group of individuals to perform low tasks, regardless of whether they were referred to as slaves or not. He further argued that assigning this status based on race was in accordance with natural law, while the presence of White wage laborers in the northern United States posed a revolutionary danger to the social class structure.

# SLAVES ACQUIRE LITERACY EDUCATION THROUGH MEANS OF RESISTANCE

Despite the legal restrictions, there were actions of resistance employed by slaves and those who were willing to teach them. In the antebellum South, despite the risks and challenges involved, numerous enslaved individuals managed to acquire literacy skills.[112] The ability to read and write was both a blessing and a curse for slaves. While owners used literacy as a means of control, resourceful slaves used it to empower themselves. Those who acquired these skills gained privacy, free time and the ability to move more freely. Some even wrote their own passes and successfully escaped from slavery. Additionally, literate slaves became teachers and played a crucial role in the underground communication network among slaves. After slavery ended, many of them used their literacy skills as a foundation for leadership positions.

The great abolitionist Frederick Douglass, a former slave himself, learned how to read and write during his enslavement. In his biography, Frederick reflected on his experience reading the speeches of Richard Sheridan and copying the letters from the pieces of timber while working in the shipyards of Baltimore, Maryland:

> *I met with one of Sheridan's mighty speeches on and in behalf of Catholic emancipation. These were choice documents to me. I read them over and over again with unabated interest. They gave tongue to interesting thoughts of my own soul, which had frequently lashed through my mind, and died away for want of utterance. The moral which I gained from the dialogue was the power of truth over the conscience of even a slaveholder. What I got from Sheridan was a bold denunciation of slavery, and a powerful vindication of human rights. The reading of these documents enabled me to utter my thoughts, and to meet the arguments brought forward to sustain slavery; but while they relieved me of one difficulty, they brought on another even more painful than the one of which I was relieved. The more I read, the more I was led to abhor and detest my enslavers. I could regard them in no other light than a band of successful robbers, who had left their homes, and gone to Africa, and stolen us from our homes, and in a strange land reduced us to slavery.*
>
> *The idea as to how I might learn to write was suggested to me by being in Durgin and Bailey's shipyard, and frequently seeing the ship carpenters, after hewing, and getting a piece of timber ready for use, write*

*on the timber the name of that part of the ship for which it was intended. When a piece of timber was intended for the larboard side, it would be marked thus—"L." When a piece was for the starboard side, it would be marked thus—"S." A piece for the larboard side forward, would be marked thus—"L.F." When a piece was for starboard side forward, it would be marked thus—"S.F." For larboard aft, it would be marked thus—"L.A." For starboard aft, it would be marked thus—"S.A." I soon learned the names of these letters and for what they were intended when placed upon a piece of timber in the shipyard. I immediately commenced copying them, and in a short time was able to make the four letters named. After that, when I met with any boy who I knew could write, I would tell him I could write as well as he. The next word would be, "I don't believe you. Let me see you try it." I would then make the letters which I had been so fortunate as to learn and ask him to beat that. In this way I got a good many lessons in writing, which it is quite possible I should never have gotten in any other way. During this time, my copybook was the board fence, brick wall, and pavement; my pen and ink was a lump of chalk. With these, I learned mainly how to write. I then commenced and continued copying the Italics in Webster's Spelling Book, until I could make them all without looking on the book. By this time, my little Master Thomas had gone to school, and learned how to write, and had written over a number of copybooks. These had been brought home, and shown to some of our near neighbors, and then laid aside. My mistress used to go to class meeting at the Wilk Street meetinghouse every Monday afternoon and leave me to take care of the house. When left thus, I used to spend the time in writing in the spaces left in Master Thomas's copybook, copying what he had written. I continued to do this until I could write a hand very similar to that of Master Thomas. Thus, after a long, tedious effort for years, I finally succeeded in learning how to write.*[113]

# The Quakers

Historians concur that literacy education among African Americans began with the Quakers. The Quakers were the initial American colonists to extend educational and religious opportunities to African Americans, based on their belief in the equality of all people and the teachings of God. They emphasized the importance of literacy among "colored" individuals to gain wisdom and salvation through the laws written in the book. Historian Carter G. Woodson argued, "Just as the colored people are indebted to the Quakers registering in 1688 the first protest against slavery in Protestant America, so are they indebted to this denomination for the earliest permanent and well-developed schools to the education of their race."[114]

The Quakers, also known as the Society of Friends, had a complex history in South Carolina.[115] Their experience was marked by fragmentation, primarily because they lived as antislavery pacifists in a slave economy and were geographically distant from other significant Quaker communities in the North. Despite these challenges, connections were upheld through visits from Friends ministers, including women, from Europe and other parts of America.[116] The Quaker community in South Carolina reached its highest point by 1800 but experienced a significant decrease as members migrated to Ohio, a state free of slavery.[117] By 1822, only a small Charleston Meeting was left, which eventually disappeared before the Civil War.[118]

# MARTHA SCHOFIELD: THE FOUNDER OF SCHOFIELD NORMAL AND INDUSTRIAL INSTITUTE

The northern Quakers' struggle to educate African Americans led to significant local effects, driven by a strong moral conviction within the sect to emulate leaders who freed their slaves. In the mid-eighteenth century, Anthony Benezet's fervent efforts, supported by Clarkson and fellow advocates, intensified the Quakers' antislavery stance and spurred them to dedicate resources toward enhancing the education of African Americans. Beyond this era, the Quakers extended their focus to improving the conditions of African Americans in various settlements. One of those settlements, Wadmalaw Island, located in Charleston County, South Carolina, birthed the vision of a young, ambitious, inspiring Quaker woman and educator from the North named Martha Schofield.

Martha was born on February 1, 1839, in Newtown, Pennsylvania, the daughter of Oliver Schofield and Mary Jackson.[119] Her parents belonged to Quaker families that had been against slavery for two generations. Martha's mother, a minister, actively campaigned against slavery by attending Quaker meetings in Maryland and Virginia. Martha received her education at home and from acquaintances and family members in the

Philadelphia region. She initiated her teaching profession in 1858 at the young age of nineteen in New York. Throughout the Civil War, she taught at a Quaker school for African American students in Philadelphia.

Martha's work on Wadmalaw Island commenced on October 16, 1865, following the arrival of herself and Mary A. Sharp, accompanied by H.A. Evans and his younger half-brother, Mr. Fisk, from New Hampshire. Their mission was to provide for and educate the 1,500 destitute African Americans left behind after Union General Sherman's March to the Sea, with only one student at their school being literate, the son of his former owner. Martha dubbed her impromptu educational institution the Garrison School, in honor of the renowned abolitionist.[120] She resided with another Caucasian woman in extremely harsh conditions, with the purpose of providing food and clothing to the vulnerable African Americans scattered across the island.

In 1866, Martha continued her efforts on Edisto Island, gaining valuable knowledge about the needs of the African American community. After a brief summer visit with her devoted family and friends in Philadelphia, Martha made the decision to forsake the comforts of home and alleviate the suffering of those on St. Helena Island. However, the hardships became too overwhelming, and Martha fell gravely ill with a severe fever. Despite her illness, Martha remained confident in her survival, as she believed there was still important work to be done. Once Martha was able to receive visitors, African American children approached her bedside, pleading for her to teach them. As she was unable to resist their requests, small classes began to gather in her sick room. Their enthusiasm served as a powerful reminder of their immense need for education.

In the early spring of 1868, Martha Schofield fell seriously ill, likely due to malaria.[121] Laura Towne, a medical doctor, cared for her, while Martha's sister Lydia was called from the North to assist. Martha had lung hemorrhages, and it appeared that her life was in danger unless she returned home to recuperate, as advised by Laura Towne. However, Martha chose to help conduct a memorial service for James Mott instead, despite her weakened state, showing her dedication to the cause of African American education in the South alongside her sister. In the evening, one of the African American men who spoke introduced a fresh perspective. He expressed that as their supportive friends from their own race, who had already made significant contributions to their progress, passed away, it was the responsibility of the African American community to contribute as much as possible toward their own education. Martha embraced this idea and put it into action. The rarity of such practices can be inferred from the fact that Dr. Attius G. Haygood of the John F. Slater Fund found it noteworthy enough to commend Martha for this approach in his 1891 report to the trustees and even suggested that other schools should adopt a similar approach.[122]

Martha Schofield relocated later in the year to Aiken, South Carolina, a town located one hundred miles inland from the coast. A small community nestled in the pine woods, Aiken, had been established three decades earlier and was beginning to be recognized as a health retreat. Martha was an instructor at a Freedmen's Bureau school, where she had limited interactions with the White community due to her support for political involvement among former slaves.

In 1871, the Freedmen's Bureau closed. Martha used a small inheritance to establish the Schofield Normal and Industrial School, a private residential school with an extended academic program and school year compared to public schools in South Carolina. The institution gained recognition for its academic excellence, as well as its diverse training programs in agriculture, home economics, industrial skills and crafts. The campus included dormitories, classrooms, a library, a chapel, a farm and craft areas, providing a comprehensive educational environment for students. Many graduates pursued careers in teaching and received state certification as college graduates upon completing the ten-year program. Martha secured funding through tuition fees, product sales and charitable donations obtained during annual trips to the North.

Martha's dedication to African American education, both in general and at her own school, kept her constantly active. She frequented Black churches, advocating for literacy and education and, in 1888, visited Salley, South Carolina, a town she described as crude.[123] The African American community in Salley was pushing for their own school, inviting Martha to speak at a meeting held at Sardis Missionary Baptist Church.[124] Upon arriving at the church with the pastor, Reverend Price, who was White, and a Mr. Daniels,[125] Martha found prominent citizens, including business owners, who were in attendance.[126] Mr. Daniels emphasized the effect of schoolhouses in Aiken County and Schofield Normal and Industrial School on the African American community. Despite facing hostility at the hotel where she stayed overnight, Martha remained composed, finding solace in writing to her sister about her inner peace amid the tension.

## MATILDA EVANS'S ACADEMIC EXPERIENCES AT SCHOFIELD NORMAL AND INDUSTRIAL INSTITUTE

Matilda received her education from her maternal grandmother and uncle until she turned thirteen. To further enhance her learning, they hired her cousin, who had been educated at the Schofield Normal and Industrial Institute in Aiken, to provide private lessons after school hours.[127] Matilda's progress was remarkable, and she excelled in Sunday school as well. When Martha Schofield spotted Matilda in Aiken, she recognized her talent and facilitated her admission to the school.[128] Matilda stayed in a private home, where her uncle delivered her provisions, and she managed her own cooking. Within a month, she became the top student in her class and maintained her diligence for four years. Matilda's hard work paid off, as she received four prizes and missed out on only one competition. Matilda's aspiration to become a physician was unexpectedly encouraged when she encountered Dr. Hannah B. Carter, a practicing physician who had graduated from the Woman's Medical College of Pennsylvania.[129] Dr. Carter became a source of inspiration for Matilda, who eagerly sought guidance on the path she needed to take to achieve her dreams. Matilda shadowed Dr. Carter, learning from her experiences and studying medical texts in her spare time.

An excerpt titled "The Story of a Negro Child's Resolve" from *The Southern Workman*, a biography written by G.S. Dickerman of Matilda when she was still alive, notes the following:

> *Matilda was at pains to be with her all that she could be, going to carry her little bag of medicine when she called on the sick, and following her movements to see what she would do, so that she might learn her ways. Dr. Carter had a few anatomical specimens and some bones to use for illustration; these were an especial delight. Then, among her books was the* Materia Medica *which Matilda was greedy to read in spare times. And from this she went out to gather specimens of trees and plants all around Aiken to bring for analysis.*[130]

After spending a year or more at Schofield, Matilda was presented with an opportunity to assist in a sickroom.[131] A professor from a college in Massachusetts had arrived in Aiken with his ailing daughter and needed someone to care for her. Matilda took on the role and gradually assumed the responsibilities of a nurse. As time passed, the tasks became more demanding as the young lady's health deteriorated, leading to her eventual passing. Following this experience, Matilda was relied on to attend to the sick within the school community. The principal, Martha Schofield, herself faced health uncertainties and occasional serious illnesses, provided Matilda with the chance to administer treatments and help her recover from critical situations.

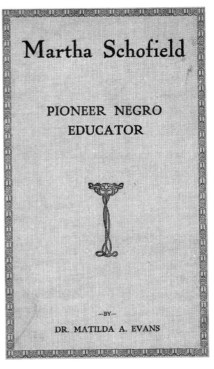

*Martha Schofield: Pioneer Negro Educator*, by Dr. Matilda A. Evans. *Courtesy of Smithsonian National Museum.*

Martha Schofield, a well-known abolitionist, White citizen and Quaker, played a significant role in Matilda's life. In fact, Matilda wrote a thought-provoking book called *Martha Schofield: Pioneer Negro Educator* to shed light on Schofield's life and legacy.[132] Matilda rightfully acknowledged Schofield's unwavering commitment to racial justice, even in the face of slander, character assassination and personal threats. However, the book also delves into broader topics such as equity in education, politics and healthcare, suggesting a larger purpose beyond honoring Schofield. Notably, historian Darlene Clark Hine suggested that Matilda used Schofield as a "ventriloquist" to express her own ideas about the current conditions faced by Black citizens, relying on the goodwill of the White physicians she worked with.[133] Additionally, the book mentions Schofield's belief in Negroland, an all-Black state aimed at separating Black citizens from White citizens and the violence associated with integration.

# MATILDA EVANS MATRICULATES AT OBERLIN COLLEGE

Matilda remained resolute in her determination. In her pursuit of higher education, she reached out to various colleges, ultimately concluding that her prospects would be most favorable at Oberlin College. It appeared that there were opportunities for disadvantaged girls to contribute toward their expenses. Composing an inquiry letter, Matilda expressed her aspiration to engage in medical missionary work among the southern population. The response she received was incredibly encouraging, prompting her to firmly commit to this endeavor. However, Matilda's acquaintances in Pennsylvania strongly objected to her chosen path. They doubted her ability to become a doctor and instead advocated for her return to South Carolina to pursue a teaching career. Using their influence, they attempted to dissuade Matilda from pursuing her plans. Despite their opposition, they did offer to provide her with a return ticket if she ever changed her mind. Undeterred, Matilda possessed her own modest savings and remained resolute in her decision. In 1887, Matilda enrolled in Oberlin and received a scholarship.[134]

Matilda's determination to overcome discouragement serves as a significant historical comparison emphasized by esteemed historian Carter G. Woodson. Woodson determined that African Americans faced discouragement from pursuing careers in the sciences due to racial discrimination from White employers and the misconception that African Americans were incapable of succeeding in scientific fields during the Jim Crow era. Woodson explained:

> *In the same way the Negro was once discouraged and dissuaded from taking up designing, drafting, architecture, engineering, and chemistry. The whites, they were told, will not employ you and your people cannot provide such opportunities. The thought of pioneering or developing the Negro to the extent that he might figure in this sphere did not dawn on those monitors of the Negroes preparing for their life's work. This tradition is still a heavy load in Negro education, and it forces many Negroes out of spheres in which they might function into those for which they may not have any aptitude.[135]*

Following a year at Oberlin, Matilda suffered a fall that left her disabled, prompting her return to Gap, where she was warmly welcomed by friends. Despite her decision to continue her college studies, Matilda's friends were

Matilda A. Evans at Oberlin College. *Courtesy of Smithsonian National Museum.*

pleased to see significant improvement in her condition. To fund her return to school, Matilda accepted a job managing the linen closet at a new summer hotel on the coast. However, upon arrival, the proprietor, upon realizing Matilda was African American, offered her a position as a chambermaid instead. She accepted the role and managed to earn eighty dollars between June and September. With this money, Matilda returned to Oberlin and remained there until December 1890, midway through her junior year. At that point, she was offered a teaching position at Haines Institute in Augusta, Georgia. After teaching there for a year, Matilda went back to Aiken and taught for two years at Schofield.[136]

Matilda's determination in pursuing her education serves as a significant historical comparison experienced by esteemed educator Booker T. Washington. Washington's pursuit of education led him to travel five hundred miles from his residence to Hampton Institute, where he graduated in 1875. When he was a student at Hampton, Washington worked as a janitor to earn money for his tuition. Washington recalled his experience:

*The sweeping of the recitation-room in the manner that I did it seems to have paved the way for me to get through Hampton. Miss Mary F. Mackie, the head teacher, offered me a position as janitor. This, of course, I gladly accepted, because it was a place where I could work out nearly all the cost of my board. The work was hard and taxing, but I stuck to it. I had a large number of rooms to care for, and had to work late in the night, while at the same time I had to rise by four o'clock in the morning, in order to build the fires and have a little time to prepare my lessons.*[137]

# THE WOMAN'S MEDICAL COLLEGE OF PENNSYLVANIA

Booker T. Washington's address titled "Speech to the Atlanta Cotton States and International Exposition" showcases a distinct viewpoint regarding the most effective approach to attain racial equality in the United States.[138] By promoting the idea of African Americans engaging in "common labor" occupations such as agriculture and domestic service, Washington garnered support from numerous White southerners, who perceived these roles as being of lower social status. In the speech, Washington argued with his position:

*To those of my race who depend on bettering their condition in a foreign land or who underestimate the importance of cultivating friendly relations with the Southern white man who is their next-door neighbor, I would say: "Cast down your bucket where you are"—cast it down, making friends in every manly way of the people of all races by whom you are surrounded. Cast it down in agriculture, mechanics, in commerce, in domestic service, and in the professions. And in this connection, it is well to bear in mind that whatever other sins the South may be called to bear, when it comes to business, pure and simple, it is in the South that the Negro is given a man's chance in the commercial world, and in nothing is this Exposition more eloquent than in emphasizing this chance. Our greatest danger is that in the great leap from slavery to freedom we may overlook the fact that the masses of us are to live by the productions of our hands, and fail to keep in mind that we shall prosper in proportion as we learn to dignify and glorify common labor and put brains and skill into the common occupations of life, shall prosper in proportion as we learn to draw the line between the superficial and the substantial, the ornamental gewgaws of life and the useful. No race can prosper till it learns that there is as much dignity in tilling a field as in writing a poem. It is at the bottom of life we must begin, and not at the top. Nor should we permit our grievances to overshadow our opportunities.*[139]

In contrast, esteemed sociologist W.E.B Du Bois positioned himself at the opposite side of the spectrum from Washington regarding the future of African American people in the United States. His perspective focused on the importance of providing higher education opportunities for African American youths and eliminating racial barriers that hindered their entry into professions such as politics, academia and medicine. These barriers were obstacles that women like Matilda faced throughout their careers. In Du Bois's acclaimed book *The Souls of Black Folk*, an essay titled "Of Mr. Booker T. Washington and Others" critiques Washington's stance:

*They advocate, with Mr. Washington, a broad system of Negro common schools supplemented by thorough industrial training; but they are surprised that a man of Mr. Washington's insight cannot see that no such educational system ever has rested or can rest on any other basis than that of the well-equipped college and university, and they insist that there is a demand for a few such institutions throughout the South to train the best of the Negro youth as teachers, professional men, and leaders.*[140]

Du Bois's vision for African Americans like Matilda who sought a professional education was realized in the founding of the Women's Medical College of Pennsylvania. Established in 1850 as the Female Medical College of Pennsylvania, this institution was the world's first medical college for women to grant them the medical doctor or MD degree.[141] Founded in Philadelphia by forward-thinking Quakers and a businessman, the college aimed to provide women with access to education and opportunities in the medical field. The college offered women the chance to teach, conduct research, manage a medical school and gain experience in a hospital setting through its women's hospital. It remained the longest-running all-women medical college in the United States until it transitioned to coeducational in 1970, admitting male students and evolving into the Medical College of Pennsylvania.[142]

The Woman's Medical College of Pennsylvania was also established shortly after the first women's rights convention in Seneca Falls, New York, which advocated for women's education and professions.[143] The college's founders, faculty and students were all part of the reform movement. Founder William J. Mullen was a philanthropist and advocate for prison reform, while other faculty members were involved in causes such as abolition and temperance.[144] The inaugural class of 1852 included Quaker women who had received comprehensive educations.[145]

The Woman's Medical College of Pennsylvania gained widespread recognition, leading to extensive coverage in newspapers across the nation. The rarity of female medical students and doctors at the time made them a subject of great interest. In 1854, the *Observer* newspaper in Feltonville, Michigan, published a favorable opinion of four women who graduated from the medical college in their community:

*We have been favored with a copy of the "Fifth Annual Announcement of the Female Medical College of Pennsylvania," located at Philadelphia. From this document we learn that the degree of Doctor was conferred on four ladies, who, we presume, intend to "set up" somewhere for the practice of their profession. We respectfully petition that some one of them should locate in our village. The doctors we have here at present, (especially one of them), being very gallant men, certainly would not object to such competition. We give our vote for a lady physician here—especially if a single lady, and therefore capable of administering a remedy for any disease of the heart that may occur.[146]*

However, even four years after the college's establishment, the opinions of female physicians published in newspapers varied significantly, with both supportive and opposing views. It is worth noting that even women authors were not unanimously in favor of the concept of women doctors. Fanny Fenn's editorial "Female Physicians," published in 1855, depicted her negative biases toward women doctors and her preference for male doctors providing prescriptions:

*FEMALE PHYSICIANS. —The* Boston Journal *strongly advocates the introduction of females into the medical profession. We consider the needle a much more appropriate weapon in the hands of woman than the scalpel or bistoury. Do you? Just suppose yourself a forlorn sick bachelor, in the upper story of some noisy boarding house, whose inmates don't care a pinch of snuff whether you conclude to die or get well. Suppose you've watched that spider in the corner weave his web, till you are quite qualified to make one yourself; suppose you have counted for the thousandth time, all the shepherdesses, distorted little dogs, and crooked trees, on the papered wall of your room; gnawed you finger nails to the very quick; and twitched your mustache till every hair stands up on its own individual responsibility. Then—suppose just as you are at the last gasp, the door opens, gently, and admits (not a great creaking pair of boots, containing an oracular, solemn M.D., grim enough to frighten you into the churchyard) but a smiling rosy cheeked, bright eyed, nice little live woman doctress yet? Well, she pushes back her curls, throws off her shawl (Venus! what a figure!) pulls off her glove, and takes your hand in those little fingers. Holy mother! How your pulse races! She looks at you so compassionately from those soft blue eyes; lays her hand on your forehead, and questions you demurely about your "symptoms," (a few of which she sees without any of your help!)*

*Then she writes a prescription with those dainty little fingers, and tells you to keep very composed and quiet, (just as if you could) smooths the tumbled quilt—arranges your pillow—shades the glaring sunlight from your aching eyes, with an instinctive knowledge of your unspoken wants; and says with the sweetest smile in the world, that she'll "call again in the morning;" and so—the fold of her dress flutters through the door; and then you crawl out of the bed the best way you can    clutch a looking glass to see what the probabilities are that you have made a favorable impression! inwardly resolving (as you replace yourself between the blankets,) not to get quite well as long as she will come to see you. Well, the upshot of it is, you have a delightful lingering attack of heart complaint! For myself, I prefer prescriptions in a masculine hand! I shan't submit my pulse to anything that wears a bonnet!*[147]

Despite reservations from authors like Fenn and other newspapers, there were men who enthusiastically supported women's right to become medical doctors. One of the founders of the Women Medical College of Pennsylvania, Dr. Joseph Longshore, supported women who desired professional education and careers in medicine. On October 4, 1850, Dr. Longshore gave a speech arguing that women possessed the qualities to become successful medical doctors and the importance of the medical college to provide educational opportunities for women:

*In order to satisfy the imperative demands, of the same laudable desire, on the part of educated and intelligent females, The Female Medical College of Pennsylvania has been instituted. The demand for this institution being so universal, so pressing, and so extensively appreciated, the Legislature of Pennsylvania…granted it a charter as broad and as liberal as any in the state, and at the same time entitled to privileges, and vested with powers equal to the most favored Medical School in the country. Where is the woman* [who is ill and in need of care], *that would not have esteemed it a high favor to have had an accomplished, educated female attendant, who from her very nature was capable of and feeling for and sympathizing with her? That the exercise of the healing art, should be monopolized solely by the male practitioner…can neither be sanctioned by humanity, justified by reason,* [nor] *approved by ordinary intelligence; prejudice, bigotry, and selfishness may dispute woman's claim to the high calling, but an enlightened liberty, and intelligent sense of justice, never.*

*That woman, from the acuteness of her perception, correctness of her observation, her cautiousness, gentleness, kindness, endurance in emergencies, conscientiousness and faithfulness to duty, is not equally, nay, by nature abundantly better qualified for most of the offices of the sick room, than man, very few will venture to contradict.…Do the women of Pennsylvania, of America, duly appreciate the relation on which they stand to this magnificent enterprise? Can they realize the vastness of this project? Have they yet become impressed with the great truth—that in this Institution is the germ of their emancipation from mental bondage and physical suffering…Will you accept or reject them? If you elect the former, then gather around us, with your influence and support—strengthen our hands—aid us in our struggle for your redemption and elevation, and millions yet unborn will rise up and call you blessed!*[148]

In 1852, Sarah Mapp Douglass became the first African American to attend the medical college.[149] She enrolled in various lecture courses at both the renowned institution and the now-defunct Penn Medical University, which ultimately sparked her passion for advocating women's health. Through her expertise in physiology and hygiene, Sarah gained recognition as an esteemed educator. Her dedication to African American women's well-being was evident, as she utilized imported "manikins" to educate them about their own bodies and promote their overall health. Additionally, Sarah delivered informative lectures on anatomy and physiology to diverse audiences, consisting of both women and men.

## Matilda Evans Matriculates at the Woman's Medical College of Pennsylvania

Upon receiving a scholarship from Alfred Jones, the bursar at Woman's Medical College of Pennsylvania, Matilda enrolled in the institution. After graduating, she reached out to Jones to request financial assistance for Melissa Thompson, a promising Black nursing student recommended by Matilda. In the letter, Matilda wrote:

> *Dear Sir: You may remember me as being the colored student to whom you gave a scholarship in 1893 to The Woman's Medical College of Pennsylvania. I graduated in the class of 1897 and came South and have built up, as I must tell you, a most enviable reputation. I have done well and have very large practice among all classes of people. I have not lost one day since I left College. I will send you under separate cover a history of my life, written by Dr. G.S. Dickerman and also a small pamphlet telling something about the work in which I am engaged outside of my general practice. It seemed when I came to Columbia that the harvest was ready and waiting for me. The obstacles I did not consider very much and I have had unlimited success. I was the first woman physician to hang out a shingle in this state and I held this honor for eight years. Since I have returned to my native state, others have been inspired and have gone to our beloved College to take degrees.*

Report card from the Woman's Medical College of Pennsylvania for M.A. Evans for her second and third years. *Courtesy of Caroliniana Library.*

*The last case is that of a colored woman, a friend of mine, named Melissa Thompson, in whose behalf I am about to write you. I have known this young woman for nine years and she has been in my nurse-training department and has helped in the dispensary at the hospital. She is a most worthy and reliable woman. Her means are quite limited; but she would be of great service if she could get a few years in medicine and surgery. I believe that she has made application for a scholarship in The Woman's Medical College of Pennsylvania and has met with some encouragement. I wish to say further that she will not be able to continue her course without some such aid being given. Her sisters, who are teachers, are sending her their earnings to help her pursue her studies. I would be greatly pleased if you can do something for her. I am sure that she will be of great service to the race and to suffering humanity. I need her greatly in my work. The poor people of her race need her. Thanking you kindly for what you did for me and hoping that you will consider her case, I remain, Yours truly, Matilda Evans, M.D.*[150]

Matilda was part of a small group of twenty-five women in the medical college, with only one other being an African American woman, Eliza Grier. The female African American graduates from this college went on to become the first of their gender and race to practice in Alabama and Mississippi. In 1897, Matilda obtained her medical doctor degree from the medical college, specializing in medicine, surgery, obstetrics, gynecology and hygiene.[151] Her graduation was announced by her mentor, Martha Schofield, during the Schofield Norman and Industrial Institute commencement address in 1897.[152]

Before going to Oberlin, Matilda took some special training in nursing, and during the second year and the summers of her college courses, she employed herself in the practice of nursing, by which she helped pay her way. She was given a scholarship to Oberlin and the medical college, which defrayed her tuition. However, while in pursuit of her education, Matilda was dependent for the most part on her own earnings for support. She engaged in many different occupations. To each one she brought a personal interest and the spirit of fidelity that made them all contribute to her education. Not only financially, but also in practical intelligence about a great many things and that efficiency prepared her for every sort of emergency. So those fifteen years, from the time Matilda entered Schofield Normal and Industrial Institute in Aiken to the day she graduated from the Women's Medical College of

Pennsylvania, were marked with vigorous progress. Twenty years from the beginning of that high resolve in the little motherless girl, brought a constant growth in character and power by the steady unfolding of her unwavering determination to create something meaningful with her life. Within the scales that determine a person's life, such valuable qualities are often hidden behind the façades of genius and luck.

# 3

# MATILDA EVANS RECEIVES HER MEDICAL LICENSE IN SOUTH CAROLINA

*The Era of Traditional Medicine in South Carolina*

The state of South Carolina's medical field was markedly distinct from the present day in nearly every aspect. Back then, the profession was unregulated nationwide, allowing anyone with the desire to practice medicine to do so, with success determined solely by market demand.

In the antebellum era, South Carolina embraced traditional medicine despite being considered unconventional, due to the scarcity of trained medical professionals until the latter half of the twentieth century.[153] Traditional medicine in South Carolina was a blend of Native American, African and European healing practices, using ingredients from general stores, patent medicines and common herbs.[154] European settlers were fascinated by the medical expertise of Native Americans, who effectively used local plants to treat illnesses and injuries. African slaves introduced their own healing methods and quickly incorporated techniques learned from Native Americans. Slaves became highly skilled in traditional medicine, leading to the common presence of midwives or female doctors on plantations. However, slaveholders were concerned about the slaves' knowledge of natural poisons, prompting the passing of a law in 1751 by the Commons House of Assembly that condemned to death any slave sharing such knowledge.[155]

# The Proposition of Medical License Laws in the United States

Following the Civil War, due to the economic challenges faced by the medical profession, a surge of medical schools emerged, leading to increased competition among doctors. In response, traditional doctors sought to organize effectively by advocating for government intervention to regulate the number and qualifications of medical practitioners. The American Medical Association, founded in 1847, representing orthodox medicine, proposed the implementation of medical licensing laws in states to control entry into the field and create a more stable economic environment for physicians by eliminating rival medical sects.[156] During the 1867 Cincinnati meeting, the association supported a resolution that urged medical professionals in different states to advocate for legislation requiring all aspiring doctors to pass an examination by a State Board of Medical Examiners to obtain a license.[157] The resolution also suggested that the board should consist of members from the State Medical Society who were not part of college faculties, initiating a movement to seek state legislatures' support in restricting the number of medical practitioners by establishing medical examining boards as the sole pathway to enter the profession in the United States.[158]

In 1894, the South Carolina legislature passed legislation signed into law by Governor Benjamin R. Tillman to establish the State Board of Medical Examiners. The law repealed the original act that provided for the appointment of county doctors to examine the diploma of doctors and surgeons in the state. The key provision in the act was that an applicant who wished to become a medical doctor was required to take and pass the examination.

# Matilda Evans Passes Her Board Certification Exams to Obtain Her Medical Licensure

An article published by the *County Record* on December 9, 1897, reported Matilda passed her board certification exams to obtain her medical licensure in South Carolina. Her performance during the exams was exceptional compared to her male counterparts. The article read:

*Columbia now has a colored woman doctor in the person of Miss Matilda Evans, who has established an office here. She graduated in medicine in Philadelphia and has considerable hospital practice. She stood the examination before the State board of medical examiners and surpassed many of the male applicants, white and colored. A woman doctor is somewhat of a novelty in this city and a colored one is an unexpected motivation in the medical profession. —*The Register.[159]

In May 1898, the South Carolina Board of Medical Examiners officially granted Matilda her medical license, and she became South Carolina's first native African American woman medical doctor.[160]

# 4

# MATILDA EVANS

*The Woman Who Made a Significant Impact on Both Her Race and the State of South Carolina Through Her Work in Healthcare*

## THE ESTABLISHMENT AND LEGACY OF TAYLOR LANE HOSPITAL

After completing her studies, she initially aspired to travel to Africa as a medical missionary but eventually chose to assist Black citizens in the United States due to the higher mortality rate among them compared to White citizens.[161] Recognizing the need for medical and sanitation education in Columbia, South Carolina, she relocated there from Philadelphia in 1897, fully aware of the challenges she would face as an African American physician in the South. In *The Southern Workman*, G.S. Dickerman conveyed his thoughts: "Few in her place would have chosen the capital of South Carolina for her field. In this home of conservatism and race prejudice, no woman hitherto had tried this profession, and no Negro physician had succeeded."[162] Dr. Evans was essential, recognizing the importance of her contribution to the community.

A professor from a college in the North sent Dr. Evans a case of valuable medicines that belonged to his sister, enabling her to provide free treatment

Dr. Matilda Evans. *Courtesy of Smithsonian National Museum.*

to patients.[163] Upon recognizing the effect of poor hygiene on common diseases, she gathered twenty women at her office to deliver lectures on practical topics, preparing them to become nurses.

After completing her first year in the city, Dr. Evans converted her own home into hospital quarters for patients and students. Subsequently, in 1901, she founded the Taylor Lane Hospital and Training School for Nurses, the first African American hospital in Columbia.[164] The hospital was established in a large old eighteen-room plantation house with ten acres of land, originally built in 1839 and remodeled in 1859, making it one of the oldest homes in the city.[165] The property also included a small house for the nurses and was managed by Dr. Evans, although owned by Mary A. Chambers.

On May 13, 1905, *The State* newspaper announced the graduation ceremonies for nursing students held at Taylor Lane:

*A large audience attended the closing exercises of the Taylor Lane Hospital and Training School for Nurses at Bethel A.M.E Church last night. Five young colored women, clothed in the conventional blue dresses, white cap white aprons and white sleeves, occupied prominent positions in front of the congregation. Two of these, Mamie A. Rustin of Greenwood and Estelle B McQuarters of Jersey City, N.J., were graduated as trained nurses after finishing a three years' course of studies at the Taylor-Lane Hospital and Training School for Nurses.*

*The address to the graduates was made by Rev. B.B. Tyler of the Episcopal church, and short addresses were made by Prof. J.R.E. Lee of Benedict college, Rev W.D. Johnson of Allen university and Rev T.W. Longwood of Durban, Natal, South Africa.*

*Dr. Matilda A Evans, the manager of the hospital, made her report to the board of corporation. She said that she had received valuable assistance from the white physicians of Columbia. She said that in four years, 1,400 people have been treated in the Taylor-Lane hospital and that 500 successful operations had been performed. She told of the large number of young colored women who have been trained as nurses in the school, which has been supported chiefly by her practice among the colored people of Columbia. Rev MG Johnson of the Presbyterian church delivered—the diploma and ministers of all the colored churches occupied seats on the platform. Good music was rendered by the students of the hospital and the entire programme were carried through with success.[166]*

City License of Columbia, 1929. *Courtesy of Smithsonian National Museum.*

Business record. *Courtesy of Smithsonian National Museum.*

Nurses outside the home of Dr. Matilda Evans, 1920s. These four nurses probably trained under or assisted Dr. Matilda Evans, whose name appears on the sign next to the mailbox in the upper left-hand side of the picture. The nurses are, *left to right*: Gretchen Evans, Sarah Green, Elizabeth Harris and Mattie Evans. In the window in the upper middle part of the photograph, observing the scene, is Dr. Evans's grandnephew Edward Evans. *Courtesy of A True Likeness.*

Taylor Lane, the first African American hospital in Columbia, served as a significant landmark for African Americans at that time. According to G.S. Dickerman in *The Southern Workman*, the hospital was supported by leading physicians and public-spirited citizens, quickly becoming a hub of beneficial activities.[167] Within the first fifteen months, 281 patients were treated, with 300 more in the following year, benefiting the entire community.[168] Wealthy White individuals sought care at the hospital, while White doctors considered it a valuable referral center. African American residents viewed it as the premier location for medical treatment and a nursing school for their daughters. Dr. Evans had a diverse patient population, catering to White women seeking discreet treatment for sensitive issues, while providing free healthcare to African American women and children, as well as addressing the lack of access to healthcare in the African American community. Dr. Evans's autobiography, *A Brief History of the Evans Clinic*, highlights her professional benevolence toward African American individuals, which not only saved lives but also earned her respect for her authority, ability and autonomy.[169]

Throughout the years Taylor Lane performed numerous surgeries related to various cases, many of which were reported in local newspapers. Some of these cases included:

> The Bamberg Herald, *October 6, 1910—John Baker, a negro, 68 years old cleft the skull of John Woodson, another negro, many years his junior, with a hatchet last night about 8 o'clock. Woodson was taken to the Taylor-Lane hospital in a dying condition. Baker made his escape. The affair occurred on Liberty Hill at a house where Baker, Woodson and the woman, whose name could not be learned, lived. At least three hours elapsed between the time the fight took place and the notification of R.D. Walker, coroner. By the time he arrived on the scene. Baker and the woman both had departed for parts unknown. Mr. Walker took the dying declaration of Woodson, which, in brief, was that he and Baker had fought over the woman and that Baker struck him with a hatchet. The wound, which is expected to prove fatal, is on the left side of the negro's head, just back of the ear. An operation was performed last night at the Taylor-Lane hospital in a desperate attempt to save his life. Woodson is*

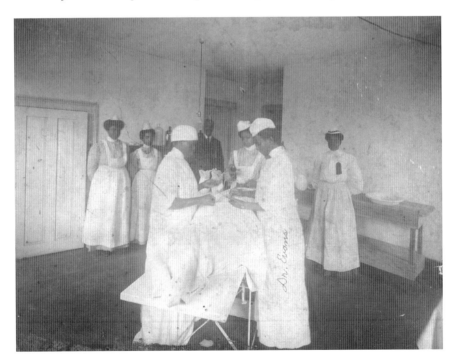

Taylor Lane Hospital operating room. *Courtesy of Smithsonian National Museum.*

*a paper hanger by trade, while Baker, the old negro who used the hatchet, is a carpenter.*[170]

The State, *January 28, 1905.—Ed Foster, a plasterer and bricklayer residing at 914 Wheat Street, suffered a severe injury when a freight train ran over his right leg in the railroad yard at the union station yesterday. The incident occurred around 7:30 PM as Foster was walking home from work; the train cars passed over his leg just above the knee, resulting in such extensive damage that amputation was required. He was taken to Taylor-Lane Hospital, where Dr. F.D. Kendall, the Southern's surgeon, performed the procedure. William Sims, who was with Foster at the time, reported that he was walking ahead and did not witness the accident, while Foster indicated he was focused on Sims trying to board the train when he was struck.*[171]

The State, *August 16, 1904—Ida Lofton, a negro woman living at 1502 Wayne street, who was burned severely three weeks ago by a lamp exploding and setting fire to her clothes, died yesterday at Taylor Lane hospital and was buried in Lower cemetery. It was reported at the time of the accident that the woman was trying to blow out a lamp and the flames got down into the oil, exploding and covering her dress with oil which caught afire and nearly burned her dress before assistance arrived. The woman's entire body, it is said, was badly burned and she was not expected to live but a few days after the accident.*[172]

The Columbia Record, *July 8th, 2010—Last Saturday, Dr. Julius H. Taylor performed: an operation on a patient at the Taylor-Lane hospital. He needed a small "live" bone to replace the one which he intended to remove and instructed Dr. Rhodes to procure a small dog or cat. At this stage of the story it is necessary to introduce court phraseology. Ed Keller, who is prosecuting Dr. Rhodes, alleged that the colored physician went to Josephine Leak, a negro woman who was caring for several small puppies which belonged to him, and told her he would like to borrow one of the terriers for a few minutes. The dog was taken to the hospital and killed, and the bone of one of the parts was used in the operation.*[173]

The State, *August 7th, 1906—Jesse Jenkins a negro man was taken to the Taylor Lane hospital Sunday night for the amputation of his right arm.*

*Jenkins was bitten by a rattlesnake in the lower part of the county about a week ago and although his life was saved, his arm was poisoned so badly that it was necessary to take it off. There are few rattlesnakes in this section of this State and the physicians of Columbia took a great deal of Interest in the case of Jenkins.*[174]

The African American community highly valued the educational significance of the hospital. Columbia provided opportunities for African American students to receive nursing training. Dr. Evans initiated a movement through Taylor Lane to increase job training access for African Americans, especially in healthcare fields promoting autonomy in the African American community. Following Taylor Lane's inspiration, Benedict College established the Pratt Nurse Training School.[175] Although Dr. Evans was intended to lead courses at the school, she was unable to do so due to her busy schedule.[176]

Dr. Evans identified numerous chances for empowering the community through Taylor Lane. She believed that the ten-acre property accompanying the building could be transformed into a farm for productive employment and communal leisure. Her knowledge of farming, particularly in tillage and stock-raising, was gained from a summer trip to Hampton.[177]

Following the initial three years, the hospital's performance began to deteriorate as financial management was delegated to subordinates, resulting in significant debt accumulation.[178] There were discussions about establishing a new hospital with a different approach, but Dr. Evans decided to sell her home and office to make the hospital her primary focus, ensuring personal oversight. Dr. Evans required staff to sign contracts committing to work for ninety days without additional compensation, emphasizing dedication to the institution. She developed plans for agricultural and patient care activities, demonstrating resilience and commitment during challenging times. Despite managing a heavy patient load with minimal remuneration, Dr. Evans's unwavering dedication to the hospital is commendable. Dr. Evans's resilience during difficult times is highlighted by G.S. Dickermann in *The Southern Workman*:

*Her time had been divided between attendance on her patients in the hospital wards and in homes, often many miles away, and occupation with plowing, planting, dairying, care of the stock, and ordering supplies for the kitchen. A number of times, when she drove out into the country to visit a patient, she returned with a small pig for her fee, and turning it loose in the pen, provided thus for her future supply of pork.…Under such a leader it is no great wonder that her associates were willing to do a great many things that are unusual. They quickly caught the spirit of doing whatever needed to be done in the house or outdoors. Cooking, laundry work, feeding the stock, milking the cows, grooming the horses, spading the garden, planting potatoes and corn, setting out cabbages, keeping down the weeds through the whole season, and then gathering in the crops in the fall—they took this as belonging to their hospital training, the same as ministering in the operating room or about the wards. And under the circumstances probably no part of their experience gave them a better training for the practical things of life than these various toils. It was a victory for every one of them to have carried the Hospital through that trying season.*[179]

After a period of uncertainty, the well-established garden yielded plentiful produce that helped reduce the hospital's expenses on food. The hospital was not only a source of income for Dr. Evans but also aimed to benefit the entire community in the long run. Dr. Evans's selfless dedication to serving others, especially in a time when medical care often came at a high cost, distinguished her from her peers. The documentation of the nurses she instructed at the institution has not all been retained. Nevertheless, historians are aware that she made efforts to educate nurses under the identities of Mattie Evans, Gretchen Evans, Sarah Green and Elizabeth Harris.[14] In addition, she sought assistance from Dr. George Bunch Sr., La Gande Guerry and John T. Duncan, who were all White doctors.[180]

Although the Taylor Lane Hospital achieved great success, the hospital had its share of controversies. On May 2, 1908, *The State* newspaper reported a rumor concerning the discovery of an infant about six months of age given to Mary Ann Clark, an African American woman who lived in Newberry, South Carolina:

*A rather sensational story concerning the Taylor Lane hospital appeared in a Newberry paper recently. The story was called forth by the so-called discovery of an Infant about six months of age which had been given to Mary Ann Clark, colored, of Newberry county by Dr Matilda A Evans, medical director of the Taylor Lane hospital. In the story appears this statement: It has the appearance of being a white child. There are no indications that there is any trace of any other blood in its veins. This is the conclusion reached by Dr Gilder and the others who saw it. Though Dr Gilder says he would not state absolutely that it is without the taint of other blood, but so far as he can judge from the examination which he made he would conclude that it is white. In the account of the finding of this infant in Newberry county appears this very suggestive interrogation: "Does this hospital also act as distributing point for infants who are not claimed by their parents?"*[181]

The Taylor Lane Hospital in Columbia was known for its outstanding reputation, and Dr. Evans was respected by both White residents and members of her own community. Therefore, the publication that aimed to tarnish the hospital's image came as a shock to many in Columbia. Dr. Evans was understandably upset by the article and promptly contacted *The State* office to request a statement be published in response:

*That which was written for the purpose of creating a sensation comes very near stating the facts in regard to the baby given Mary A Clark, a respectable old colored woman of Newberry county. It is easy for those looking for sensation to find it. "You will note that Dr Glider would not say absolutely that the child is without the taint of other blood but he seems inclined to pronounce it" a white child. He, however, erred sadly on the right side by leaving it with Mary Clark, who signed an agreement assuring us that the child would never come to want, and that if at any time she was unable to care for it she would return it to me in order that it may be placed in an orphans' asylum. The city of Columbia has presented me with a bright little girl and I shall be pleased to find a good respectable home for her. "Rest assured that should any one envy Mary Clark her treasure and prove to me that they are more able to support this child than she, I will say 'Amen'." "If it takes a sixteenth part of a drop of negro blood to make a negro then my fair Crucita Alberta Juanita Clark is nestling under the shadow or the shelter proscribed for her and her race by the laws of the State of South Carolina and the manners and customs of her people. (Signed) "M A Evans M D "Medical Director Taylor Lane Hospital."*[182]

Dr. Evans believed that the Taylor Lane Hospital and her work in the state had been unfairly portrayed in the article, causing a significant sense of injustice:

*"I think the people of Columbia know me too well," she said, "to put any credence in an article containing such insinuations. Any one could have easily obtained the truth about this child which was given to the old woman In Newberry county. The child's mother is as much of a negro as I am and I don't see how any one could have imagined for an instant that I would give a white child to a negro. Frequently infants are given me when the mother dies or when the parents are unable to care for it, and I do what I can toward finding good homes for all of them. These children are not born at the Taylor Lane hospital as might he easily interpreted by reading the article referred to. As stated the city of Columbia through the chief of police has given me a bright little girl and I will do what I can to find a suitable home for It." Dr Evans is held in high esteem by the members of the medical profession in Columbia, and, as stated above, by the public generally. She is regarded as a woman of upright principles and is known as a sympathetic and philanthropic worker among the sick, infirm and poor people of her race. The publication referred to is regarded by the friends of Dr. Evans and of the Taylor Lane hospital as very unfortunate, to say the least.*[183]

On January 23, 1909, *The State* newspaper reported the case of H. Van Buren, an African American who interned at Taylor Lane Hospital, who was charged with practicing medicine without a license by the State Board of Medical Examiners. *The State* offered witnesses to show that Van Buren signed prescriptions at the dictation of Dr. Evans. Van Buren was tried in court and was acquitted.[184]

The popularity and positive reputation of Taylor Lane Hospital prompted several African American community leaders to form a committee to discuss the idea of building a hospital for African Americans in Columbia. The committed was chaired by Dr. W.D. Chappelle, who served as president of Allen University at the time.[185] On Monday afternoon, April 10, 1911, Allen University hosted an interest meeting for Columbia's African American citizens that included students and faculty to discuss the building of the hospital and praised the work of Dr. Evans:

*The Coppin hall of Allen university was pretty well filled with an audience composed of the faculty and students of Allen and colored citizens from the city on Monday afternoon. The occasion was a mass meeting in the interest of the Taylor Lane colored hospital. Dr. W.D. Chappelle, president of Allen, presided, and Prof. C.H. Rembert acted as secretary. A committee on resolutions was appointed as follows: Rev. M.G. Johnson, Prof. J.W. Morris, and Rev. E.A.P. Cheek. Dr. Chappelle, on taking the chair, stated the object of the meeting. He referred to the great need of a hospital for colored people in Columbia, and the good and noble work that Dr. Matilda Evans is doing in the work of establishing such an institution. The Rev. M.G. Johnson, Dr. Matilda Evans, Dr. Francis C. Van Garken of Philadelphia, Miss Margaret Eastburn of Aiken made strong speeches in behalf of the enterprise of building a hospital in Columbia for colored people. Dr. Van Garken and Miss Eastburn are white ladies from the North. Dr. Van Garken urged the colored people to help themselves, and then others will come to their rescue and help them. The keynote of her address was: "Build a hospital by yourselves, of yourselves, and for yourselves." "But," said the speaker, "the good people of Columbia and of the North will help you." Short addresses were made by Joseph T. Pelot, C. Perrine, Z.E.*[186]

The committee passed a resolution commending the work of Dr. Evans and efforts to provide medical services to poor African Americans, lauded her character of integrity and service and encouraged Dr. Evans's friends for support:

*"Resolved, That the people of this city and community hold Dr. Evans in the very highest esteem possible, believing in her integrity as a lady worthy of the respect of everybody.*

*"Resolved further, That we have the very highest and unfaltering confidence in her as a citizen and as a physician.*

*"Resolved further, That we believe that she has done all that a woman could do to establish in this city a place to relieve the poor and suffering people, and that it would be a calamity to this people for the work to fail now.*

*"Resolved further, That we believe that she is the proper person for the management of such an institution, coupled with a board of directors or trustees.*

*"Be it resolved, That a committee be appointed by this meeting to draw up a set of resolutions or to write a strong letter to the friends of Dr. Evans in the interest of this movement." The committee on resolutions was made permanent and Prof. R.E. Brogdon was added to it. This committee will prepare an address to the people of Columbia asking their aid in the building of a hospital for the colored people of Columbia.*[187]

Regrettably, the Taylor Lane Hospital and Training School for Nurses was destroyed in a fire on May 10, 1911, at approximately 2:30 p.m., as reported by the *Bamberg Herald*. The fire was believed to have originated from a faulty flue and resulted in a $5,000 loss with only $1,200 insurance. The only items salvaged were a few pieces of furniture, bed clothing and a piano. There was a fire the month before, but it was extinguished before causing significant damage. At the time of the fire, there were ten patients in the hospital, who were promptly evacuated by nurses with the help of rural policemen R.S. Hipp and W.D. Grimesly. Recovering patients were sent home, and those awaiting surgery were taken to Dr. Evans's farm.

As far as Dr. Evans is concerned, her devotion to work at Taylor Lane Hospital is a legacy of service, empathy and ingenuity. Dr. Evans's work at the hospital garnered praised from male doctors, including a well-known surgeon who was quoted in *The State* newspaper:

> *The following recommendation from one of the best and most widely known surgeons in South Carolina speaks for itself: "I have known Dr. Evans for several years, being closely identified with the work done at the Taylor Lane hospital for colored people, of which she is superintendent. I know of my own knowledge that the good accomplished for needy negro people not only of Columbia, but throughout the entire State, has been incalculable, from a verbal statement, to give an expression of the great amount of good that has been accomplished or how great the need of money. It is my honest belief that Columbia furnishes a field for such work unexcelled anywhere. Dr. M.A. Evans has shown signal ability as superintendent of such an institution. There is in connection with the hospital a training school for nurses, which as likewise been productive of much good by furnishing employment and means of livelihood for many deserving negro girls."*[188]

# VILLA NOVA

Dr. Evans assumed control of Villa Nova, a mineral spring water company, during this period, offering its products at her clinic to alleviate kidney issues in her patients. An advertisement was published in *The Southern Indicator* on July 25, 1914:

*Kidney complaint disappears like the dew before the rising sun by the use of the now famous mineral spring water owned by Dr. Matilda A. Evans at Villa Nova. Villa Nova is located about three miles from Columbia on the Two Notch road, on an eminence commanding a splendid view for miles of the surrounding country. Just under the brow of this eminence, there gushes a flow of pure mineral water that has proven a boon to hundreds of persons suffering from kidney complaints. What this water*

Dr. Evans and an unidentified individual. *Courtesy of the family of Dr. Matilda Evans.*

*has done for others similarly affected, it will do for you. This health giving elixir can be had by calling on or addressing John B. Evans* [Dr. Evans's son] *and David Cannon, Managers. The water is on sale at 1019 Lady Street and will be delivered to any address in the city.*[189]

# THE ESTABLISHMENT AND LEGACY OF THE NEGRO HEALTH ASSOCIATION OF SOUTH CAROLINA

In 1916, Dr. Evans helped establish the Negro Health Association of South Carolina, which was also known as the South Carolina Good Health Association.[190] This organization focused on providing public health services through visiting nurses. The organization declared and petitioned for their incorporation under state law:

*The undersigned declarants and petitioners Matilda A Evans, MD, Columbia, S.C., Butler W Nance, Columbia S.C., JC White, Columbia S.C., being two or more of the officers or agents appointed to supervise or manage the affairs of The Negro Health Association of South Carolina which has been duly and regularly organized for the purposes hereinafter to be set forth do affirm and declare: That at a meeting of the aforesaid organization held pursuant to the bylaws or regulations of the said organization they were authorized and directed to apply for incorporation. That the said organization holds or desires to hold property in common for a religious, educational, social, fraternal, charitable or other eleemosynary purpose or any two or more of said purposes and is not organized for the purpose of profit or gain to the members otherwise than is above stated or for the insurance of life, health, accident! or property. The said declarants and petitioners further declare and affirm: First. Their names and residences are as above given. Second. The name of the proposed Corporation is The Negro Health Association of South Carolina. Third. The place at which it proposes to have its headquarters or to be located is Columbia, S.C, No 502 Sumter St. Fourth. The purpose of the said proposed corporation is the promotion of the public health of the negroes of South Carolina; operate Saint Luke Hospital and Training School for Nurses. Fifth. The names and residences of all managers, trustees, directors, or other officers, is as follows: Matilda A Evans, M.D, Columbia, S.C, secretary, president. Butler W Nance, Columbia S.C*

St. Luke's Hospital and Evans Sanitorium. *Courtesy of Smithsonian National Museum.*

Nursing staff at St. Luke's Hospital and Evans Sanitorium. *Courtesy of Smithsonian National Museum.*

Dr. Evans and staff in front of St. Luke's Hospital and Evans Sanitorium. *Courtesy of Smithsonian National Museum.*

*first vice president. J.C. White, Columbia, S.C., secretary. Sixth. That they desire to be incorporated in perpetuity. Wherefore your petitioners pray that the secretary of state do issue to the aforesaid (Matilda A Evans, Butler W Nance and J C White) Certificate of Incorporation, with all the rights, powers, privileges and immunities and subject to all the limitations and liabilities conferred by an act of the general assembly of South Carolina entitled: "An Act to provide for the incorporation of religious, educational, social, fraternal or charitable, churches, lodges, societies, associations, or companies, and for amending the charters of those already formed and to be formed" approved February 19, A.D. 1900, and other provisions of law. Given under our hands and seals this 12ᵗʰ day of June, A.D. 1916. MATILDA A EVANS, BUTLER W NANCE, J CL WHITE.*[191]

A significant initiative was launched by the organization, aiming not only to provide aid to the ill and solace to the afflicted but also to improve health standards within African American households. Consequently, a health campaign was initiated in Columbia specifically for the African American community, with the goal of reducing the high mortality rate and enhancing overall well-being. The association was convinced that cultivating good health practices would help prevent the transmission of germs.

The Negro Health Association of South Carolina actively supported St. Luke Hospital and Evans Sanatorium, which was Columbia's second African American hospital in the city's history, supervised by Dr. Evans.[192] The association's efforts were fueled by charity, leading both Whites and African Americans to recognize the positive effect on Columbia and actively respond to its needs. Dr. Evans was confident that improving the living conditions of cooks and laundresses would enhance the city's overall health, prompting collaboration for the success of the initiative. Dr. Evans expressed great enthusiasm for the progress and outcomes achieved through the work.

St. Luke Hospital's primary facility was adequately furnished, featuring a modern operating room with ample light and ventilation. The hospital was frequented by the Caucasian doctors of the city, who performed a substantial amount of work there. It boasted fourteen rooms with a total of twenty beds, with a particular focus on surgical procedures and treatment for various illnesses. The hospital's operations were primarily funded through charitable means, as the promoters aimed to assure the people of Columbia that it was not a corrupt scheme and that their support was genuinely appreciated.

In 1916, Dr. Evans established *The Negro Health Journal of South Carolina*, a weekly newspaper that was sold for $0.05 per copy (equivalent to $1.48 today) and had an annual subscription fee of $0.50 (equivalent to $14.83 today).[193] One of the articles in the newspaper focused on preventing typhoid fever through simple methods, health cooperation and addressing low wages as a societal issue.[194] Dr. Evans encouraged readers to petition local governments for better environmental conditions to prevent the spread of the disease and offered tips on basic hygiene practices. She emphasized the importance of avoiding dead animal bodies, reducing manure piles, ensuring food screenings and reporting cases to health authorities for disease control. Dr. Evans also appealed to readers using a religion-based cultural understanding, linking hygiene practices to the love of God and the importance of caring for one's own soul as God's image.

In 1917, upon the United States' entry into World War I, the Negro Health Association of South Carolina proposed the federal government use St. Luke Hospital as a public health clinic and a training school for African American nurses. On September 1, 1918, the *Sunday Record* published a letter written by the organization publicly pleading the federal government utilize St. Luke:

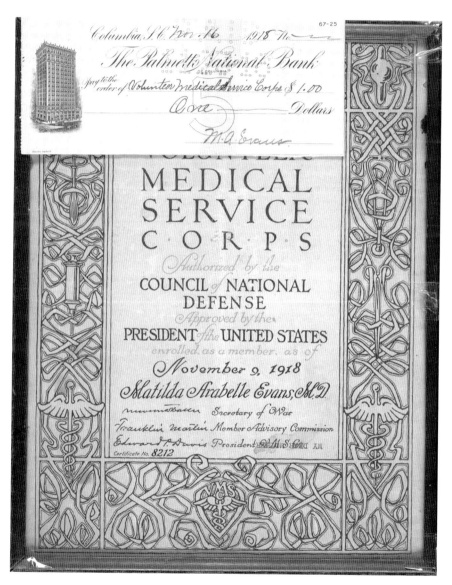

Authorization by the Council of National Defense. *Courtesy of Smithsonian National Museum.*

*The executive committee of the Negro Health association of South Carolina does hereby offer to the United States government through the South Carolina Council of Defense, the use of St. Luke's hospital, 502 Sumter Street, Columbia S.C, for a public health clinic and war nurse training school for colored army nurses and the purpose of building up avenues of usefulness in the creation of our army. We wish to tender our utilities to be directed and utilized under any improvements or improved methods under army regulations. This association realizes and has been impressed by observation that our army is in very great need of colored nurses and that our civilian population in in need of clerical service. It is our most humble wish that we may be able to be of some service to our country. In this capacity, St Luke's has already been made a recruiting depot for colored nurses and is meeting with success in this line. Our association is at the service of the Council of Defense through our president Dr M.A. Evans, and the chairman of our executive committee the Rev E.S. Willett, for the propagation of the gospel of health throughout the state—E.S. Secretary for Committee The colored women of the State are enrolling in the United States student nurse reserve and should the plans as outlined by St Luke's hospital materialize, this will enable the women to be trained in the State for this war service.*[195]

The primary objective of the weekly newspaper was to disseminate crucial public health information to the African American community. However, it also contained some of Dr. Evans's political viewpoints and appeals for action.[196] In one excerpt, Dr. Evans opposes capitalist exploitation, contending that neither the African American worker living in unsanitary conditions and consuming spoiled food nor the White landlord benefits from low wages. She employed a combination of personal storytelling and statistical data to convey her argument: "There is no way to calculate the moral cost borne by the residents of these homes and consumers of this food, in addition to the financial cost, for the privilege of living inexpensively. South Carolina, with a Negro population of less than 1,000, spends $10,000,000 on medical care for Negro sickness and death, and over $1,000,000 on undertakers." Dr. Evans also indirectly discussed health disparities, focusing on the significant racial gap in tuberculosis deaths between Black and White patients during her era. She emphasized the importance of cooperation between both races for effective solutions to public health issues, as highlighted in *The Negro Health Journal*.

# THE AMERICAN RED CROSS

In 1917, the *Columbia Record* reported that Dr. Evans, along with several prominent African American citizens, had formed the Negro Branch of the American Red Cross in Columbia:

> *Negro Red Cross Branch Is Active (Written for* The Record*) The colored people of Columbia who met three weeks ago and organized themselves into a Red Cross unit have at last perfected their organization with the Rev JC White as chairman; Dr Matilda A Evans, vice chairman; Maggie Belle Penn, secretary; Rosa B Gaten, assistant secretary; Rev RW Baylor, treasurer. The following committees have been appointed: Educational, WH Thomas, chairman; finance, Dr. F.B. Johnson, chairman Membership; Dr JH Goodwin, chairman Supplies, James A Brigham, chairman, distribution; Ellen Woods, graduate nurse of the government hospital, chairman relief, Geo B Dwellie, chairman. The organization met at Zion Baptist church Monday night and voted unanimously to become a branch association to the Columbia chapter at of which Dr JA Hayne is the chairman. The negro branch will send all their reports to Washington through the Columbia chapter and will cooperate with it in every move for the relief of the American soldier especially and for mankind in general the world over. The colored branch has an enrollment of 120 members and reported the same to Mrs. Weston this morning with money to be forwarded to Washington. The executive committee met this morning in the office of Dr JH Goodwin and got out the captains for teamwork of this city. They expect to raise $2000 and turn over same to the Columbia chapter by the middle of next week. Captains who will push the work have not all been named a partial list follows: Rev JC White, W II Thomas, James A Brigman. Rev RW Baylor, Geo B Dwellie, Dr. JH Goodwin, JB Green, Dr. FB Johnson, Rosa B. Oaten, M.B. Penn, Dr. M.A. Evans, Elvira Veal, Eva B. Rutherford.*[197]

On October 12, 1918, *The State* newspaper reported over five thousand cases of influenza in Columbia that devastated households and businesses.[198] The influenza epidemic led to health and food crisis in the city. Some individuals experienced different outcomes, but everyone was affected by the influenza outbreak. The city did not conduct a thorough survey, and there were reported instances of individuals in need of care risking their lives due to lack of access to medicine and proper nourishment. While some families were ill and had no one to care for them, others had only children to meet their needs. Numerous stores operated with reduced staff, some employees stayed home to care for sick family members and others were forced to shut down completely. Cooks fell ill, making it nearly impossible to find any kind of assistance.

The influenza epidemic had a direct effect on women and girls in Columbia. The local Southern Bell Telephone Company experienced a significant loss of forty-one female employees out of a workforce of one hundred due to the influenza outbreak. This resulted in a severe reduction of the company's service and doubled the workload for the remaining employees. In one case, an African American girl, homeless and destitute, suffered with pneumonia.

To combat the influenza epidemic among Columbia's African American population, the Red Cross employed the services of Dr. Evans to recruit African American workers for the Red Cross to provide nursing aid to those who were suffering. A recruiting call for African American volunteers was announced in *The State* on October 12, 1918:

> *Call to Negro Red Cross Workers, To All Negro Red Cross Workers of Columbia: You are hereby notified to meet at the headquarters of the Odd Fellows' building, Assembly Street, this morning at 10:30 o'clock for the purpose of making a survey of the entire city of Columbia and report the number of sick among the negroes to the State board of health. This is important, and you are expected to answer to your names. This notice takes in all workers of the Palmetto branch of the Columbia Chapter also the members of the Union Baptist branch. J.C. White, Chairman.*[199]

## CHILD DESERTION CASE

On May 25, 1923, the *Columbia Record* reported a newborn baby had been left on the steps of Dr. Evans's home on a Thursday night:

> *An infant three or four days old was found in the steps of the residence of Dr Matilda Evans on the Two-Notch road Thursday night. Dr Evans said she had returned from the Waverley tabernacle, where a*

*colored revival has been under way and was informed by members of her household that at about 9 o'clock cries of an infant attracted their attention to the porch. Investigation revealed the presence of a baby girl. The infant had been carefully wrapped in neat and clean garments and its head rested upon a small pillow filled with absorbent cotton. The infant appears to be healthy, Dr. Evans said. At present no steps will be taken to place the child in a permanent home as Dr Evans said she desired to keep a watch over her young charge to determine her state of health and nationality and to obtain other details that will be of importance when steps to find her a home have been undertaken. The person who discovered the infant on the porch recalled hearing an automobile pass or atop near the house a short time before the cries of the infant attracted their attention. The child left on Dr Evans' porch Thursday night is the third instance in which she has been the involuntary recipient of a baby. The circumstances of the desertion of the two other babies were practically similar to the latest case. Good homes were found by Dr. Evans for the two other little charges. The baby figuring is the latest case, Dr. Evans said, is of fair complexion has light hair and blue eyes.*[200]

# THE BIRTH OF A CLINIC IDEA

Over the years, Dr. Evans selflessly served her people by tending to their physical suffering, listening to their cries of anguish, witnessing their poor health conditions and often seeing them deprived of modern medical treatment due to extreme poverty. This sparked a generous spirit within her, leading to the beginning of a groundbreaking initiative.

Dr. Evans endeavored to share with others her deep passion for establishing a clinic for the community, despite receiving minimal support and understanding from those in influential positions. Due to her unwavering faith in God, trust in her community and the validity of her argument, she decided to approach the Secretary of the State Board of Health. The secretary attentively listened to Dr. Evans and, recognizing the value of her narrative, wholeheartedly agreed to assist in any way he could. Subsequently, he followed through on his promise, as will be elaborated on later.

Dr. Evans was pleased to have the support of Mrs. Olympia Harris, a skilled and diligent graduate nurse, who provided valuable service in arranging a meeting with Reverend J.P. Reeder, the pastor of Zion Baptist Church in Columbia.[41] Following the conference, it was agreed that a Child's Clinic would be held in the church's Sunday School department, where children would receive examinations and free vaccinations if needed. Dr. Evans aimed to assess the effectiveness of her strategies and persuade others she reached out to about the viability and requirements of a clinic, as well as the validity of her approach. Her intention was to conduct a basic health check and survey on the health status of preschool-aged children and administer vaccinations to those who had not yet followed the legal requirements.

The State Board of Health secretary was to provide the vaccines and any other necessary items. Plans were arranged for an average of two hundred individuals per day during the allocated time frame. However, Dr. Evans was unaware that a larger number than expected were eagerly anticipating the day when they would receive the distressing news about their malnourished and weak physical state.

The day began with clear and sunny skies. Dr. Evans brought along her own team of private assistants from the office, as well as a group of ten public school teachers and a few additional volunteers. The time had come, and over seven hundred people had already gathered outside the entrance. They were welcomed inside, and Dr. Evans, along with her team, began to examine them. They came from all over the city, making it difficult for the workers to keep up with registration. By the end of the first day, more than seven hundred had been registered.[201] The following day, children and adults crowded the entrance, blocking the streets and bringing traffic to a halt. The police investigated to determine the cause.

The sight of the large crowd, with 90 percent of them suffering from various ailments, was truly distressing. It would have surely convinced even the most stubborn skeptic of the necessity of the plan. One incident stands out: Mr. W.C. Johnson, a businessman and temporary president of the organization, was so overwhelmed by the crowd at the clinic that he felt compelled to seek out Dr. Evans for help, threatening to resign from his position if the situation was not addressed. Dr. Evans arrived at the church to find the situation dire, with those in charge doing their best to help.

Numerous children came back seeking something they thought they deserved. For example, a young girl who had already been examined, approached Dr. Evans and requested, "Please ma'am, my mother said, could you check my mouth, eyes, throat, and feel my heart." By the end of the

96

session, more than four thousand children had undergone inspection. The overwhelming number of people seeking examinations led to the depletion of vaccine supply from the State Board of Health.

Dr. Evans's friends were concerned about her health due to her intense interest, prompting them to advise her to take a break. Despite feeling inspired and not wanting to leave, she eventually agreed to take a trip. It was later discovered that she went to New York City to study and visit the most advanced clinics in the country, which turned out to be a highly successful endeavor.[202]

## The Establishment and Legacy of the Evans Clinic

While she was away, the movement gained momentum due to the high interest. Mr. Johnson, as mentioned earlier, proceeded with great enthusiasm and secured a building at 1235 Harden Street, which was destined to become the clinic location.[203] He personally paid the first month's rent and covered the cost of having the building cleaned and painted appropriately.

On July 6, 1930, Dr. Evans established the Evans Clinic Association, which ran the Evans Clinic (also known as Columbia Clinic) as a nonprofit organization approved by the State Board of Health.[204] The clinic, with various departments overseen by specialists, was praised for its contributions to disease prevention, health and education. Dr. Evans conceived the idea for the clinic after witnessing the hardships faced by African American individuals. Upon Dr. Evans's return to the South, she was accompanied to the site of the clinic and formally presented with the keys, marking her homecoming.[205] Overwhelmed with gratitude, tears filled her eyes as others joined in celebrating the realization of the vision she had held for years. Dr. H.H. Cooper, a prominent and accomplished dentist in Columbia, stepped up to support Dr. Evans's plans with genuine interest. Not only did he offer his services, but he also generously provided the essential equipment for the dental department, effectively and diligently meeting the needs of the children.

In an interview with *The State* in discussing the operations of the recently established medical facility, Dr. Evans quoted:

*The health conditions among our people in the city is alarming. I was distressed to find so many children underweight, under nourished, and actually suffering for the lack of some simple treatment that would give better health. Before we were able to set up our work we had to educate people up to the idea of having such an institution. We went from church to church and from school to school and as a result we find more work to do than we can handle. I believe the people will support the new clinic nicely. Already friends have paid the rent for two months, given furniture and other equipment and have assured us that in the near future we may be able to add to the work a day nursery. We wish the public to know that services at the clinic is free. This work is not intended to interfere with the practice of any of our physicians, as every parent will be free to have his child treated by his family physician if he desires, and, only in cases where the parent or guardian is not able or does not have a family physician will the clinic serve in treating the juvenile patients.*[206]

The Columbia community expressed deep gratitude toward Dr. Evans for her dedicated efforts in establishing the Evans Clinic. On December 1930, Olympia Harris organized a celebration to honor the clinic's thirtieth anniversary in Columbia, where she aimed to improve healthcare for African American citizens.[207] Unfortunately, Dr. Evans was unable to attend due to ptomaine poisoning, but the event proceeded with heartfelt speeches. Dr. James P. Reeder blessed Dr. Evans, recognizing her as a true servant of God for her selfless service to the community. Mr. and Mrs. Roberts, Mrs. James and Mrs. H.H. Cooper also delivered impromptu speeches during the event.

Despite the inadequate funding, Dr. Evans proposed a highly practical plan to her interim board, outlining her next course of action: establishing a child habit clinic and kindergarten, conducting health education lectures and organizing lectures and demonstrations on child welfare and hygiene.[208] Additionally, she planned to hold prenatal clinics twice a week. Children continued to arrive throughout the day, and Olympia Harris, who had received specialized clinical training in New York City, aided. They often left early to work at the clinic until ten o'clock in the morning, after which Dr. Evans would leave her assistant in charge and rush to her private office to attend to impatient clients from all over South Carolina. In the afternoon, she continued to see patients until late in the evening.

Dr. Evans and her assistant frequently traveled to different towns and cities in the state for speaking engagements and to examine hundreds of children, ultimately examining several thousand through the Clinic Extension Service. J.E. Dickson, a State Farm demonstration agent, deserved much credit for the success of the Clinical Extension Service. He consistently made sure to include this important work in his programs, allowing for effective work in various communities in Richland County, such as Eastover and Gadsden.[209]

Social workers, along with Dr. Evans and her team, conducted a comprehensive health survey in all crowded areas of Columbia, ensuring that the data was properly documented for future use. Simultaneously, the temporary board members convened a meeting to establish a permanent executive board, secure a vehicle for the nurse and discuss strategies for obtaining financial support to sustain the ongoing work. Various departments were available to provide services, including physiotherapy, otolaryngology, dentistry, urology, obstetrics and gynecology, prenatal and pediatric care, as well as a child behavior clinic and mental health services.[210] Ruth Bynum collaborated with a group of young men from Benedict College called the IPTs in the social service department.

The Evans Clinic received financial support from the Columbia City Council ($4,900.02).[211] Unfortunately, the clinic suffered greatly due to the overall lack of funds. The clinic was forced to sell their facility. To raise money, the clinic leadership began initiating fundraising activities and advocacy campaigns to purchase a new facility.

In May 1933, the Evans Clinic organized a large gathering at Bethel Church to launch a membership campaign aimed at fundraising.[212] The event featured African American and White speakers, as well as musical performances. Another membership campaign event was planned during the gathering, coinciding with Florence Nightingale's birthday, to kick off a drive to raise $2,660 for essential expenses needed for the clinic's operation and survival.[213]

Frank F. Whilden, a prominent individual in Columbia, South Carolina, was recognized for his vivid memories of important historical occurrences. He recounted in detail the burning of Columbia in the Civil War and the Charleston earthquake of 1886, providing a unique personal insight into these events in South Carolina's past. On June 27, 1933, Whilden, who was one of the White members of the clinic board, wrote a letter to the editor of *The State* appealing for aid to support the Evans Clinic, foreshadowing the future of the clinic:

*To the Editor of* The State: *Again I am constrained to appeal through your valuable columns for aid for the work at the Evans clinic. With most intense interest I read the report in Friday's State of Dr. Ella Oppenheim, how clearly, from a scientific standpoint, she has pictured the conditions prevailing in our city among the poor Negro children. I quote from one who speaks with experience and authority: Washington, June 22-(UP)-The United States may be on the highroad out of the business depression, but the effects of the grueling years since 1929 are only beginning to show themselves on the nation's youth, the children's bureau of the department of labor says in five, ten, or perhaps 15 years, the ugly sins poverty, malnutrition and wretched living conditions probably still will be visible, Dr. Ella Oppenheimer, who has made an extensive study of child health, tells the United Press today. It is not too late, she believes, to avoid such a condition, Prompt mobilization of preventive medical agencies and a wider distribution of relief might make it possible to heal most of the wounds. Otherwise, she thinks, there will an army of the sickly veterans injured in a war in which no shot was fired. Future Dark. "There is no doubt." Doctor Oppenheimer said, "that we have built trouble for future. Which way the trend will go in the next five years no one can say. Continuation of present conditions will make it grow worse.*

*Reports from health centers in several of the large cities indicate a striking increase malnutrition among children not old enough to go to school." Worst Danger Cuts: The worst danger, Doctor Oppenheimer feels, is that the agencies that are charged with the care of children are becoming sorely pressed for money and have been forced to curtail their activities, as well as state health services. She said, "[We] have in many instances had severe cuts in appropriations. There is no question but that this letdown in child health work can be very serious." As one specific danger signal, Doctor Oppenheimer mentioned the situation in a large city, where a child was brought in suffering from tubercular meningitis. Doctors said their facilities made it impossible to the added patient. "That child," he said. "is going to die anyway. There is nothing that can be done." This woman evidently has a mother heart, and her admonition should appeal to us. While these conditions cannot be entirely eliminated, yet they can in a large measure be ministered to by an organized body, with facilities for such work, provided the necessary funds are available. We are grateful to those who answered our former appeal through these columns; the need is still very pressing. Again, we appeal more help, clothing for children, milk, food and money. I could tell you of appealing stories of this work that have come under my observation. I appeal to your generosity. FRANK F. WHILDEN, Member of the Board.*[214]

On August 15, 1933, Whilden wrote another letter to the editor of *The State* asking for donations with the goal of raising $2,000 for maintenance for the Evans Clinic:

*Must Raise Two Thousand Dollars For Maintenance of Evans Clinic To the Editor of* The State*: May I be permitted once again to intrude on your generosity? As I looked at the picture in the issue of* The State *of August 9 and read the story of "Undernourished Go to Camp," my old heart rejoiced for the kindness of those who make this work possible, but—these are all white children; what about the blacks, who are just as needy, and even more so? There is one institution that is doing fine work in aiding this class in our community, the Evans clinic, under the management of an interracial board. The struggle to survive is a hard one, indeed. To keep this worthy charity running at minimum expense until next spring will require $2,000, and this must come from the voluntary contributions of citizens. Today a band of 120 workers, whites and blacks organized for a campaign, will go out into our community and endeavor to raise this amount. If you are called on, please, in the name of humanity respond as liberally as you can, and if the committee does not reach you, please send in your dollar, or more, as your heart moves you to give. We received no appropriation from the state this year; the city has been kind to the work, but could not do very much. Mail your donation to the writer at 509 Duke avenue, or to the Evans Clinic, Harden street. Acknowledgment will be made. We desire this worthy charity to continue but it cannot unless you come to our aid. FRANK F. WHILDEN, Member of the Board.*[215]

On November 15, 1933, Whilden wrote a favorable op-ed column praising the work of the Evans Clinic and encouraging the public to support the work of the clinic:

*There exist in our Capital City and suburbs* [a] *class of people little known and less thought of. I refer to the class of Negroes who are poor financially and physically; their abodes are almost uninhabitable, with minimum comforts of home furnishings; their food is of the plainest kind. In these homes are children undernourished, with diseased bodies and no funds for physicians' care, medicine, food or nurse; they simply have "an existence." Health conditions among such Negro children were exceedingly poor before the depression now they are almost indescribable. There is an institution in the city on Harden street established by a kindly-hearted Negro physician, Dr Matilda Evans, and she has maintained here for several years [a] "clinic" for these poor and unfortunate. Children are brought here daily, hungry, undernourished, poorly clad; here expectant mothers come for advice and help and to beg for [a] cup of tea or coffee or a cup of milk or little medicine. This work has been carried on largely by Doctor Evans and a band of faithful colored friends, but they can give but little to sustain their splendid benevolence. A short time ago their work was regularly organized and the institution chartered and put under the management of an interracial board. The officers are Negroes; the president is Theodore Youngblood (president of an insurance company); vice presidents, James Wakefield and Prof T.L. Duckett of Benedict college; secretary, Marion Dixon; treasurer, Alberta Simonds. The white members of the board are: Bishop K.G. Finlay, Mrs. M.O.J. Kreps, Frank F Whilden, Mrs. Waddell Pratt, and Mrs. Mary Sanborn of Aiken. Dr. Hy Monteith, a young Negro physician and surgeon, gives liberally of his time and ability, a trained nurse is on duty part time. Dr Leon Wakefield is the attending dentist, and work is being carried on under the most adverse conditions. Yet the records show thousands have been treated and benefited. The greatest need today is for money to meet rent of building, water, lights, telephone medicines. Professional services are rendered free. You are invited to visit the clinic on Harden street and to see for yourself the urgent need. Milk, clothing, comforts of any kind are acceptable. These people are struggling to do their part among their own race, but they need the help of their white friends. Any inquiry addressed to any member of the board will receive attention. Read the words of our Lord in Matthew chapter 25, verses 34 to 46, and may God open your hearts and pocketbooks to respond! Frank F Whilden.*[216]

The Evans Clinic secured a new location in Columbia on 2014 Taylor Street by Christmas 1933.[217] The newly constructed facility included areas designated for laboratory experiments, administrative tasks, a kitchen for the nutritionist, surgical suites and individual rooms for patients requiring specialized care. The clinic goal of securing a new facility encouraged Dr. Evans to spur charitable initiatives to support the well-being of poor African American children in Columbia. On November 30, 1933, the clinic hosted a Thanksgiving dinner for several hundred African American parents and children. The guests enjoyed a satisfying dinner and were provided with fruit to take home while underprivileged children also received a complimentary Thanksgiving meal at Evans Clinic. In talking to a group of people who visited the institution during the occasion, they stated that Dr. Evans was enthusiastic and encouraged the success of the Thanksgiving meal:

> *Doctor Evans spent yesterday at the clinic. In talking to a group of people visiting the institution she said: "For four years we have been carrying on this work and I believe it is about sold to the people of Columbia. We have been encouraged by both white and Negro people and thousands of needy children have been given aid in health, food, clothing and the like since we started the work. For our Thanksgiving dinner for the children we have donations from several sources. Among them I may mention the Sunday school department of the Washington Street Methodist church, a few clubs among the white people and also donations from Benedict College. Besides helping the needy, the Evans clinic is trying to foster what I have always stood for, and that is a spirit of good will between the two races."*[218]

On Christmas Day, December 25, 1933, the Evans Clinic provided clothing and food to eighty-one children. Many of the donations, including food, fruit and clothing, were brought to the clinic on Christmas Eve by the Washington Street Junior Sunday School class.[219] This generous act resulted in numerous baskets of fruits, food and clothing being presented to needy and destitute children, bringing the total number of needy cases reached by the clinic workers in 1933 to 1,100. Dr. Evans was convinced that her charitable work was a calling from God, and she was optimistic that the people of Columbia would recognize the importance of the clinic and provide the necessary funds for a permanent facility to help the less fortunate.

The Evans Clinic's achievements drew national recognition and gained the backing of renowned African American scientist Dr. George Washington Carver. Clinic board member Frank F. Whilden wrote a letter to the editor of *The State* newspaper on January 25, 1934, promoting a fundraising event organized by the Evans Clinic, highlighting Dr. Carver as the guest speaker and praising his work and character:

> *To the Editor of* The State*: The Evans clinic a benevolent institution under the management of an interracial board is struggling to keep alive supported by the work and gifts of the Negro people of this city and donations for the city itself and we are hoping from the state also this year. Friends of the clinic frequently give entertainments to raise funds to carry on the work and they need the help of white friends. A movie and interesting entertainment is scheduled for Friday February 2 at 8pm at the clinic house, 2014 Taylor street. It will be an evening with Doctor Carver, at which time a talk will be given on the life works of this great man. One of his special products is known as "peanut wafers" which will be made by expert and sanitary hands and wrapped in sanitary paper and with each package there will be enclosed a recipe by Doctor Carver how to make these wafers. The price of admission is only ten cents. Dr George Washington Carver was born on a farm in Missouri and took the name of his owner. At the close of the Confederate war he and his mother were stolen by a band of raiders. He was traded off for a horse valued at $300. His mother disappeared, and his father was dead. He had a craving for knowledge and began his self taught education with an old Blue Back spelling book which he mastered. His young life began in the laundry business by which he paid his way through school. Dr Booker T Washington heard of him and brought him to Tuskegee institute in Alabama where he has been ever since as a professor. Thomas A Edison offered this "brother wizard" a fine salary and contract for five years to be in his laboratory but he said no! He has been elected a member of the Royal Society of Arts in London England. Few in America have been so honored. Doctor Carver has made himself famous as a scientist, naturalist, painter, educator and has produced by his test tubes 100 products of sweet potatoes, 145 from peanuts, 95 from pecans, also a paint from the soil. On one occasion the ways and means committee of the house of representatives in Washington was considering the question of tariff on peanuts. They heard a number of prominent speakers for ten minutes each[;] finally this Negro was called and for ten minutes he modestly produced his evidence then sat down. The committee cried "More! More!" and Doctor Carver was recalled and spoke for one hour and 45 minutes. As a result, peanuts were written in the tariff. Doctor Carver is an earnest humble Christian. When asked, "What do*

*you attribute your wonderful success to?", he always replies "To God."*
*Papers, magazines and books have been written about this great man, yet*
*he continues as humble as ever. His health is fine. Very active, he rises at*
*4 a.m., walks in the woods and communes with God and nature. Several*
*of his former pupils are living in this city. Through the kindness of the*
*Gibson drug store, Main and Laurel Streets and Murtiashaw's Shoe*
*Repair shop on Main street tickets have been left at these places for sale.*
*It is hoped that our white friends will buy these tickets to aid this much*
*needed benevolent. FRANK F. WHILDEN.[220]*

On August 22, 1934, the Evans Clinic sponsored an event at Columbia's Township Auditorium featuring legendary African American jazz singer and vocalist Cab Calloway and his famous Cotton Club Orchestra.[221] Even though Calloway's "Hi-De-Ho" was well known and his orchestra had played on Columbia screens in various films and shorts, the clinic's event marked Calloway's initial live performance in Columbia.

Dr. Evans's adopted son, John B. Evans, organized the large event for both White and African American attendees, with half of the balcony seating reserved for White spectators and the first floor for the dancers. All had the opportunity to enjoy some of the finest music ever played in Columbia.[222] Calloway and his orchestra performed so well that the clinic requested him and his group to come play again.

On January 23, 1935. Dr. Evans published her fifth annual report to *The State* about the success of the Evans Clinic and thanked the public for their continuous support for the clinic, despite the challenges and obstacles they encountered:

*Dr. Matilda A. Evans, founder of Taylor Lane hospital in 1905*
*and founder of Evans Clinic in 1930, makes a plea to and thanks*
*the generous public for a continuous support of the clinic which has*
*weathered the storm of depression and is pretty well established as*
*one of the useful institutions in the city. Doctor Evans has written*
*her fifth annual report of the clinic, which is being sent to members*
*of the board of directors of the institution and other friends. In her*
*report she gives an account of the work done this year and includes a*
*resume of the most important things done by the institutions thorough*
*it workers during the past five years. Three persons are on the staff of*
*Evans Clinic. These persons, under the guidance of Doctor Evans,*
*have made a survey of the actual condition of underprivileged people*

*in the city and in certain sections of the county. Many of cases have been brought to the clinic and given medical help, food, clothing and free examination. "The Evans Clinic has rendered assistance to more than 12,000 persons in the past five years and in many instances has found work for people whose greatest need was employment whereby those dependent on them could be given some kind of shelter, food, and clothing," Doctor Evans said in telling of her work among the people through the Evans Clinic.*[223]

# 5

# MATILDA EVANS

*Her Roles as a Civic Advocate and Entrepreneur*

## THE ATLANTA RACE MASSACRE OF 1906 AND THE COLUMBIA RACE CONFERENCE OF 1907

On the Saturday afternoon of September 22, 1906, the Atlanta newspapers released reports of four alleged assaults on local White women, all of which were never proven.[224] Throughout the day, extra editions of the newspapers were published containing sensationalized details and increasingly provocative language. As a result, thousands of White men and boys gathered in downtown Atlanta to protest. Despite efforts from city leaders, including Mayor James G. Woodward, to pacify the growing angry crowds, their attempts were unsuccessful.

As the sun began to set, the once peaceful crowd transformed into a violent mob, wreaking havoc on the streets of Decatur, Pryor and Central Avenue until well past midnight.[225] The central business district became a battleground as hundreds of African Americans fell victim to the mob's relentless attacks. African American–owned businesses were targeted in the chaos, with the windows of Alonzo Herndon's barbershop being shattered. Herndon had closed early and was absent from the scene. However, another barbershop across the street was not as fortunate, as the barbers inside fell victim to the rioters' brutality and lost their lives. The streetcars were also targeted by the crowd, who entered the streetcars and assaulted African

American men and women. The situation escalated to the point where the militia had to be called in around midnight, leading to the suspension of streetcar service. Despite this intervention, the mob continued to show no signs of relenting. It was only after a heavy rain began to fall around 2:00 a.m. that the crowd finally dispersed. At that point, Atlanta was under the control of the state militia.

On September 23, the Atlanta newspapers published a report detailing the deployment of the state militia to quell the mob, as well as the assertion that African Americans were no longer posing a threat to the White population following the violent events of the previous Saturday night.[226] The police, armed with rifles, and the militia were tasked with patrolling the streets and safeguarding White-owned property, while African Americans, in fear of a potential return of the mob, clandestinely acquired weapons to defend themselves. Despite the law enforcement presence, White vigilante groups managed to infiltrate certain Black neighborhoods, prompting African Americans to defend their homes and successfully repel the encroachments.

On the morning of Monday, September 24, a gathering of African Americans took place in Brownsville, a neighborhood situated just two miles south of downtown Atlanta.[227] This community was notable for being the location of the historically Black Clark College, which later became Clark Atlanta University, as well as Gammon Theological Seminary. The group that had assembled in Brownsville was reported to be heavily armed, causing concern among the Fulton County police, who were made aware of the situation. Fearing the possibility of a violent confrontation, the police decided to act and conducted a raid on the neighborhood.

Unfortunately, this led to a shootout in which one officer lost his life. Following the tragic incident, authorities responded by dispatching three companies of heavily armed militia to Brownsville.[228] Their mission was to disarm the individuals involved in the gathering and restore order to the community. As a result, over 250 African American men were arrested, and their weapons were confiscated. Despite these efforts, sporadic clashes continued to occur throughout the day, further escalating tensions in the area.

The violent uprising played a significant role in the approval of a statewide ban on alcohol and the imposition of limitations on Black people's right to vote by the year 1908.[229] It undermined the credibility of the conciliatory approach advocated by Booker T. Washington among Black leaders, paving the way for a shift toward more assertive methods in the pursuit of racial equality.[230] This shift was exemplified by W.E.B. Du Bois, who penned a poignant poem titled "The Litany of Atlanta" following the riot, thereby lending greater legitimacy to the use of forceful tactics in the fight for justice.[231]

In her account of the racial massacre in Atlanta, Dr. Evans asserted that if African Americans were not subjected to discrimination in their urban occupations and were actually encouraged to invest in and improve their homes—rather than facing discouragement and obstacles such as White people refusing to rent homes built by African American labor— the potential for racial tension and riots like the one in Atlanta in 1906 could be significantly reduced.[232] In her view, this would empower African Americans to surpass any other race that the southern White people might try to attract to settle in the region. Over time, Dr. Evans believed African Americans could potentially outshine even those claiming to have the purest Aryan blood in terms of their moral conduct, as they were already surpassing them in the field of agriculture.[233] This shift in dynamics could lead to a more harmonious and prosperous society, benefiting all members of the community.

Dr. Evans's perspectives aligned with the view of a famous African American clergyman named Richard Carroll. Carroll, a prominent figure in South Carolina's history, was born in Bamberg County on November 2, 1860.[234] Despite being born into slavery, Carroll managed to rise above his circumstances and become one of the most influential African Americans in the state during the early twentieth century.[235] During his mid-teens, Carroll's life took a significant turn when he attended a revival near Denmark, South Carolina, led by Reverend A.W. Lamar, who was the secretary-treasurer of the South Carolina Baptist Convention. It was at this revival that Carroll experienced a religious conversion that would shape the course of his life. Inspired by his newfound faith, Carroll began to consider a career in the ministry.[236] However, faced with limited professional and educational opportunities in his rural community, Carroll made the decision to move to Columbia to attend Benedict Institute, later known as Benedict College, where he would further his education and pursue his calling to serve as a religious leader in his community.[237]

Carroll's approach to addressing the challenges faced by the African American community was heavily influenced by the principles of Booker T. Washington's Tuskegee Machine.[238] He strongly opposed the social activism of W.E.B. Du Bois's Niagara Movement and instead emphasized the importance of self-help, economic development and moral uplift as the most effective means to address the "Negro Problem." Through his speeches and writings, Carroll discouraged political agitation, advised against Black migration to northern cities and sought to appeal to the paternalistic sentiments of his White supporters.[239] His rhetoric, centered on racial self-help and political conservatism, found a receptive audience among White newspapers, particularly William E. Gonzales's *State* in Columbia.

In 1907, Carroll orchestrated the inaugural annual conference on race relations in Columbia, drawing African American leaders nationwide and influential White South Carolinians.[240] This conference was convened in response to the recent unrest in Atlanta, aiming to foster improved relations between the races. While it may seem unnecessary for Columbia specifically, the discussions were geared toward shaping the long-term future rather than addressing immediate concerns. During the conference, Booker T. Washington delivered a speech in which he expressed his support for Carroll's efforts.[241] Washington's endorsement of Carroll's work was seen as a significant moment in the event, highlighting the importance of collaboration and recognition within the community.

Dr. Evans participated in the conference where she, alongside Celia D. Sazon, delivered a presentation focusing on the theme of "The Negro Woman's Burden."[242] The aim of their presentation was to shed light on the struggles faced by African American women due to the intertwined issues of racism and sexism. During their presentation, both Dr. Evans and Sazon emphasized the multifaceted nature of these challenges, highlighting how they affected various aspects of women's lives in areas such as education, employment, healthcare and social interactions. They were cognizant of the far-reaching consequences of these challenges, recognizing how they perpetuated systemic disadvantages and created barriers to opportunities for African American women. Dr. Evans and Sazon underscored the importance of acknowledging and actively addressing these challenges, urging conference attendees to work toward dismantling the oppressive systems that uphold these inequalities. By raising awareness and taking concrete steps to alleviate the burdens faced by African American women, the attendees of the conference could play a pivotal role in fostering a more just and equitable society for all individuals.

During the conference, Washington made a visit to Dr. Evans at Taylor Lane Hospital.[243] In his autobiography, *Up From Slavery*, Washington eloquently described the influential work of Dr. Evans:

*She has been unusually successful. Among her patients are the descendants of the family to which her grandmother and mother had belonged as slaves. At the same time, she is on the best terms with all the doctors in the town, White and Black, who have assisted her in establishing and maintain the Taylor-Lane Hospital, of which she is the founder and has the entire management.*[244]

# LINDENWOOD PARK

In 1922, Dr. Evans managed her own farm, Lindenwood Park, where she raised chickens, cows, pigeons, vegetables and fruit trees.[245] The park was located three and a half miles from Two Notch Road in Columbia. The farm not only provided employment opportunities through farming but also served as a recreational space for the public. The park featured picnic grounds, games and a swimming pool area offering swimming lessons. An auditorium with a seating capacity of four thousand and a lunch counter were available, where farm-grown products were sold to visitors. Various

Lindenwood Park. *Courtesy of A True Likeness.*

artists from the state performed at the park, and occasional events were organized for farmers to give lectures on the importance of farming. Regular advertisements were placed in African American newspapers to promote Lindenwood Park.

This advertisement was featured in *The Southern Indicator* on August 12, 1922:

> GET THE HABIT. *Take a dip in the beautiful Swimming Pool at Lindenwood Park. The park is splendid with natural beauty—grass covered hills, shade trees, walks and drives and a fine Spring of pure sparkling spring water—"A thing of beauty is a joy forever." The Pond with a great inflow of pure water from the high hills above is the greatest in the State of South Carolina. On the bank of this beautiful pond are 44 bathing houses, lockers to accommodate patrons. Manager in charge—from 10 A.M. until 11 P.M. A Lunch Counter is to be maintained where good EATS will be in operation at all times. Menu—Fine fat, juicy chicken, Eggs on toast, Salads, Berries, all Lindenwood Park's own products. A FINE BIG AUDITORIUM that will well accommodate 4,000 is in readiness for service in case of rains or storms. One of the most beautifully fascinating places in the whole world is Lindenwood Park on a moonlight night. CLASSIC MUSIC EVERY NIGHT BY Mr. John B. Evans, who has recently returned from Oberlin Conservatory of Music where he made a specialty of violin, will direct the music. BIG CROWDS AND MUCH MERRIMENT EVERY AFTERNOON AND EVENING New Swimming Classes are being formed—Same will meet on Monday and Friday afternoons at the park.*[246]

The Farmer's Picnic & Barbeque took place at the park on Wednesday, August 16, 1922, marking the end of the planting season.[247] Distinguished speakers discussed farm-related subjects and recreational activities and allowed farmers to showcase and sell their products. Families were urged to bring their children for a learning experience about agriculture.

# NEGRO STATE FAIR ASSOCIATION

In early October 1925, in the recent annual stockholders meeting of the Negro State Fair Association at Bethel AME Church in Columbia, Dr. J.H. Goodwin was reelected president, with Green Jackson as secretary,

Thomas A. Williams as treasurer and T.L. Duckett as superintendent.[248] Dr. Evans was elected to the executive committee as an at-large member responsible for organizing the annual Negro State Fair in South Carolina, promoting diversity and community representation. R.W. Westberry, secretary of the fair, emphasized the importance of participation in Dr. Evans's *Negro Health Journal*.[249]

The Negro State Fair in Columbia began on October 27, 1925, with an exciting program planned for the entire week.[250] The fairgrounds were bustling with preparations for what was expected to be a highly successful event organized by the African American community, featuring a wide range of attractions and exhibits to attract large crowds. The fair started on Tuesday with a special focus on "Baby and Mothers' Day," which included a baby show and other activities. Wednesday was known as "Derby Day" with entertainment, derby races and various attractions. Thursday was designated as "Everybody's Day" with a football game and a boxing show as the main sporting events. Friday was dedicated to "School Day," featuring a football match between Booker T. Washington and Wilson High School teams. The fair ended on Saturday with thrilling automobile, motorcycle and bicycle races, providing an exciting conclusion to what was a memorable and eventful week for all participants.

## CHURCH ACTIVITIES

In 1924, Dr. Evans delivered a speech during the Thirty-Sixth Annual Session of the Women Department of the Missionary Educational Convention of the African American Baptist Denomination of South Carolina at Second Calvary Baptist Church in Columbia.[251] The focus of her presentation was health.[252] Throughout the session, a total of fifteen classes were organized, consisting of both local scholars and visitors. The visitors took charge of leading the lessons, aiming to familiarize the Sunday school attendees with the teaching techniques commonly employed in different Sunday schools throughout the state. The classes were structured in such a way that a diverse group of individuals, including both locals and visitors, could come together to share their knowledge and expertise. By having the visitors lead the lessons, the attendees were exposed to a variety of teaching methods commonly used in Sunday schools across the state. The interaction between the local scholars and visitors created a dynamic learning environment, allowing for a rich exchange of ideas and experiences. This approach not only introduced the attendees to new teaching techniques but also fostered a sense of collaboration and community among the participants.

Dr. Evans was a key figure in the Columbia African American churches, especially on June 8, 1926, when she took part in a pre-convention meeting at Zion Baptist Church with other prominent African American leaders to prepare for the National Baptist Sunday School Congress Convention.[253] During the meeting, Reverend J. Dean Crain urged Reverend J.C. White, the coordinator of the convention, to ensure its success by emphasizing cleanliness. He also commended both Whites and African Americans for their support of Reverend White's efforts:

> All of the speakers at the Sunday meeting encouraged White in his endeavor to make the congress a success. Mr. Crain said: "When you suffer, we suffer with you. When the cook is sick at home it is a serious handicap to us. We cannot live independent of each other. Every right-thinking white person in Columbia wants all of you to be somebody. The coming to Columbia of this great crowd of people will help the city. You have been asked to clean up your premises and put your home in sanitary condition. This will help you. We need to emphasize the use of soap and water more and to love to have clean surroundings. The convention is going to bring to you some new ideals that will help you in your own life and endeavors. I'm glad to see a many white and Negro people supporting the Rev. White in this great movement to provide entertainment for the congress. We need a spacious coliseum owned by the city so that we can make Columbia one of the greatest convention cities in all of the South."[254]

The Thirty-Sixth Annual Session on June 9, 1926, was a significant event reported on by *The State*, with more than one thousand delegates gathering to participate.[255] Attendees traveled from various parts of the country to be part of this convention, which was highlighted as the largest gathering of African Americans in the South and specifically in Columbia. The convention headquarters were situated at 1027 Washington Street within the city's African American business district, adding to the historical importance of the event. Dr. Evans played a crucial role in overseeing the coordination of women's work related to the arrival and management of the delegates during the convention.[256] This responsibility entrusted to Dr. Evans showcased the importance of organization and leadership in ensuring the smooth functioning of such a large-scale gathering.[257] The presence of dedicated individuals like Dr. Evans contributed to the overall success and impact of the convention in bringing together a diverse group of delegates for meaningful discussions and interactions.[258]

## African American Business Organizations

Dr. Evans, in her writings, documented the existence of almost fifty thousand African American–owned businesses, encompassing a wide range of industries such as banking, insurance, manufacturing, funeral services and healthcare.[259] The collective annual revenue generated by these enterprises exceeded $1 billion. Additionally, the African American community boasted a total of sixty-six banks with a combined capital and surplus amounting to over $2 million.[260]

The South Carolina State Negro Business League (SCSNBL) was the state affiliate of Booker T. Washington's National Negro Business League (NNBL).[261] Washington established the NNBL in Boston in 1900 to promote African American business growth, and it functioned as a chamber of commerce for the community. The NNBL aimed to foster economic development, self-reliance, racial pride and self-help among African Americans. Additionally, the NNBL played a crucial role in inspiring the formation of various other African American organizations, such as the National Negro Bankers' Association, the National Negro Funeral Directors' Association, the National Negro Bar Association, the National Association of Negro Insurance Men and the National Negro Press Association. A diverse group of professionals, including doctors, lawyers, bankers, barbers and farmers, actively participated in the league.

On July 18, 1920, *The State* covered the meeting of the South Carolina State Negro Business League at the Phyllis Wheatley Club in Columbia on Washington Street.[262] The purpose of the meeting was to establish a network of African American–owned banks throughout South Carolina. Dr. Evans was the sole woman among the attendees, which included influential figures like H.E. Lindsay, I.S. Leevy and R.W. Westberry, who expressed support for the league's initiative.[263]

Dr. Evans was the medical examiner for the Mutual Relief and Benevolent Association, also known as South Carolina Mutual, the oldest African American insurance company in South Carolina.[264] An article about the association's history and work was published in the *Columbia Record* on October 22, 1916:

> *The Mutual Relief and Benevolent Association of South Carolina or "The South Carolina Mutual" is the oldest negro insurance company in the state. The company [is] enjoying a good business. The company mottoes is "a company that is 1,000 strong the credit of the negroes." The officers are: J.H. Fordham, Orangeburg, president; A.W Simpkins, vice-president; James H. Goode, secretary-treasurer and general manager. The board of directors consists of the following members: A.W. Simpkins, S.S. Youngblood, J.J Durham, H. Culberson, W.H. Thomas, William Blake and H.C. Cooper. Dr. Matilda A. Evans is the medical examiner. The home office of the company is in Columbia over which J.H. Goode has charge. Six clerks are employed in the office. There are one hundred agents in the state. For the period, January 1 to June 30, 1916, $3,026.87 was paid in death claims. The present general manager is carrying forward the work of the company well. He was one of the founders of the company and has been engaged as agent and director since that time.*
>
> *The company lends money to its policyholders, on good security, for buying of homes. The scale of weekly payments runs from five cents up and a large benefit, in proportion to the amount invested, and is paid upon sickness and death. The company has passed the experimental age. It is operated on a sound financial basis and deserves the patronage of the negro race. A campaign is now on in which agents are given prizes for securing the largest number of new and permanent members. This contest will close with the year and success is being gained by the campaign. One of the founders of the company who helped to build it up was the late Rev. A.F. Dunbar, who was a leader of the negro race in the state. He instilled in his associates, who are business and professional negro men, the principles of a good company and to his efforts is due much of the credit of the concern. The promoters of the company believe that the work is but beginning and optimistic over the success of the company in the future.*[265]

# SOUTH CAROLINA AFRICAN AMERICAN WORLD WAR I MONUMENT COMMITTEE

During World War I, African American soldiers from South Carolina made a notable contribution to the war effort. *The Official Roster of South Carolina Soldiers, Sailors, and Marines in the World War*, published in 1929, documents the individuals from the state who answered the president's call upon the United States' entry into the conflict.[266] This roster includes approximately twenty-seven thousand Black men, accounting for one-seventh of the adult Black male population in South Carolina.[267] The 371st Regiment, an all-Black unit led by White officers, displayed remarkable bravery during the final stages of the war in France, showcasing their valor and commitment.[268] For many African American residents of South Carolina, participation in World War I represented an opportunity to assert their citizenship and advocate for meaningful change at home, inspired by President Woodrow Wilson's appeal to "make the world safe for democracy."

In 1919, the Negro Race Conference convened at Second Calvary Baptist Church in Columbia, where it passed a resolution addressed to the mayor of Columbia, the governor of South Carolina and the state legislature, advocating for the construction of a memorial monument honoring African American soldiers from South Carolina who valiantly fought and perished in World War I:

> *The night session at Second Calvary Baptist Church. R.J Crockett of Rock Hill offered the following resolution as a memorial, which was adopted: "We, the undersigned committee of the Race Conference, assembled in annual session, hereby petition the mayor of the city of Columbia, the governor of South Carolina and legislature and citizens of the State at large in the following memorial:*
>
> *"Whereas, a large number of the faithful negroes in the State, who responded to the call of the governor and president of the United States, willingly sacrificing their lives for their country; and*
>
> *"Whereas, These lives were given for the common good of humanity; therefore*
> *"Be it resolved that the negroes in Race Conference assembled here pray that these precious lives, so freely given be memorialized by the erection of a monument in the capital city of the state of South Carolina, with fitting subscription telling future generations that they did die for the liberty of humanity and the peace of the world.*

*"Further, be it resolved that his excellency, Gov. R.A. Cooper and the legislature make an appropriation to duplicate the funds subscribed by the negroes and public at large to pay for said memorial, to be erected in some suitable public place to tell of their heroic sacrifices made for world freedom."*[269]

The resolution was drafted by the conference committee members, consisting of men and Dr. Evans, the sole woman on the committee. In the conference, a memorial monument committee was established with R.W. Westbury of Sumter chosen as chairman and I.S. Leevy of Columbia as vice chairman. Dr. Evans played a role in appointing a large committee to develop plans for the memorial and organize a fundraising campaign to collect $100,000 from African Americans for the project.[270]

## Safeguarding Columbia's African American Women

On July 4, 1917, the *Columbia Record* detailed a gathering of African American physicians and ministers at Ladson Presbyterian Church on Sumter Street in Columbia.[271] The purpose of the meeting was to discuss ways to protect the moral integrity of young African American men and women in the city. It was noted that the establishment of the cantonment could also lead to increased immorality among young African American women, prompting plans for their safeguarding at future meetings.

Dr. Evans, a participant in the meeting, proposed the closure of African American dance halls operating near Main Street in the city.[272] Additionally, she suggested that churches schedule their services in the afternoons to prevent young African Americans from being out at night. These suggestions were well received by the attendees.

# QUIETING THE UPROAR OF THE DEMONSTRATION AGAINST THE ENLISTMENT OF AFRICAN AMERICAN MALES IN THE MILITARY AMID WORLD WAR I

On April 5, 1917, *The State* documented that representatives of African Americans from Columbia and other parts of the state met with Governor Manning to offer the military services of the race to the chief executive of South Carolina and the president of the United States.[273] Resolutions of great significance were passed at a mass meeting of African Americans at the First Calvary Baptist Church, marking the first formal discussion of the race's role in the impending world war.[274] Similar actions had already been taken by African Americans in North Carolina and Florida. The resolutions stated that in this meeting, it was believed that the government, whether state or national, must promptly arrange for military training and instruction for willing members of our community.[275] This would enable them to offer effective and valuable service when enlisted.

During the meeting, there was a clear division among attendees regarding the involvement of African Americans in the war, with some expressing their dissatisfaction openly. The chairman, Reverend Richard Carroll, DD, consistently called for opinions from everyone present, which led to a fervent protest from the audience against one of the most passionate speakers.[276] The crowd, visibly shaken with anger, interrupted the speaker before he could fully articulate his argument, particularly when he provocatively stated, "The white folks have the Winchesters, and you haven't even a little popgun. They'll not ask you whether you want to enlist. They'll just take you out and shoot you, if you don't."[277]

Chaos erupted from a single sentence, prompting numerous attendees to stand up in protest.[278] Despite repeated efforts to resume speaking, the speaker's voice was drowned out by a cacophony of clapping, hissing and insults directed at him. Moments later, the same defiant words were hurled back at the audience, who responded with enthusiastic approval. The speaker later revealed that L.A. Hawkins, whom he accused of causing disruption, was upset because he declined to purchase real estate Hawkins had been trying to sell.[279]

Dr. Evans, in attendance at the gathering, restored harmony by stepping forward and initiating with a shaky voice, the patriotic American hymn written in 1831 by Samuel Francis Smith, "My Country, Tis of Thee."[280] Immediately, the agitated crowd, previously moving its limbs and shouting in disarray, rose up and united in the melodic cadence.

## FAMILY BUSINESSES

Dr. Evans, together with her adopted son and business manager, John B. Evans, and her niece, Jessie L.H. Trottie, successfully operated various business ventures in Columbia. She also owned a leisure property called Cottage Inn, which served as a recreational venue for the youth, promoting community cohesion among the Black residents of Waverly.[281]

Jessie Trottie Hill, niece of Dr. Matilda Evans, who taught at the Waverly School in Columbia, South Carolina. *Courtesy of the family of Dr. Matilda Evans.*

In 1930, Dr. Evans established a pharmaceutical firm named Evesco Products, which was granted a charter to manufacture, purchase and sell pharmaceuticals and related goods.[282] The company was initially capitalized at $5,000, with Dr. Evans acting as president and treasurer, Jessie as vice president and secretary and John as the third director.[283]

# 6
# MATILDA EVANS

## *In Her Last Days*

## DR. EVANS IS HONORED BY THE NATIONAL MEDICAL ASSOCIATION

In 1935, Dr. Evans, a physician with thirty-seven years of experience in Columbia, was celebrated with a testimonial banquet by the Congaree Medical Society, marking her as the first African American woman in South Carolina to be recognized by the National Medical Association.[284] The event took place at Dr. W.D. Chappelle's residence.

*The State* newspaper released an article on March 3, 1935, covering the testimonial banquet held in honor of Dr. Evans:

> *Matilda A. Evans, a Black female physician with 37 years of experience in practicing medicine in Columbia, was honored with a testimonial banquet by the Congaree Medical Society on Friday evening at Dr. W.D. Chappelle's residence. On the program for five minutes talks were Dr. Julian Stuart who spoke* [on] *Doctor Evans as founder and superintendent of Taylor Lane Hospital and Training school for nurses; Dr. Robert W. Mance, who spoke on Doctor Evans as a citizen; Dr. Frank Johnson on Doctor Evans as a physician; Elise Jenkins, wife of Dr. D.K. Jenkins, on her as a foster mother for 27 children she had educated and Ada Cooper, wife of Dr. H.H. Cooper, on Doctor Evans as a benefactor. Visiting guests, Doctor Pickett*

*of Camden and Dr. E.A.E. Huggins of Greenville, also spoke. Doctor Pickett presented Doctor Evans with a bequest [sic] of white carnations. Other remarks were made by Doctors D.K. Jenkins, Durham Counts: W.E. Thomas, A.N. Jenkins, and W.D. Chappelle, Dr. H.D. Montieth, president [of] the Congaree Medical society, presented her with set of silver candlesticks on behalf of the society.*

*Doctor Evans is a graduate of the Woman Medical College of Philadelphia, 1897, She began practice in Columbia 37 years ago, as the first Negro woman physician in South Carolina. Beside founding the Taylor Lane hospital in 1901, she is founder and head of the Evans Clinic, is past president of the Congaree Medical society, the Palmetto State Medical Society and has served as the regional president of National Medical association [and] was editor of the* Negro Health Journal *when it was first published in 1916. Her interest in the education of children and other similar activities have been one of her foremost hobbies, though she herself has [not] had children of her own nor has been married.*[285]

## DR. EVANS'S DEATH AND MEMORY

On November 17, 1935, Dr. Matilda Arabella Evans, a trailblazing African American physician from South Carolina, passed away at her residence in Columbia at four o'clock in the afternoon.[286] She suffered a medical emergency in Kershaw County while attending the funeral of a former employee. Dr. Evans was quickly brought back to Columbia and passed away soon after. Funeral services took place on Tuesday afternoon, November 19, 1935, at 3:30 p.m. at St. Luke's Episcopal Church, with interment scheduled at Palmetto Cemetery.[287]

Dr. Evans was born in Charleston, South Carolina, and grew up in the Kitchings Mill community of Aiken County.[288] Dr. Evans pursued her education at the Scholfield Normal and Industrial Institute in Aiken, followed by Oberlin College in Ohio, and ultimately earned her medical degree from the Woman's Medical College of Pennsylvania.

Dr. Evans not only fulfilled her regular responsibilities in her field but also managed a clinic that offered complimentary medical care to disadvantaged African American children in the urban area. Her significant impact in this aspect has received widespread recognition. Over a span of thirty-seven years, Dr. Evans devoted herself to the medical field in Columbia, establishing the Taylor Lane Hospital and the St. Luke's Training School for Nurses located at the intersection of Taylor Street and Two Notch Road in Columbia. Taylor Lane Hospital holds the distinction of being the first African American hospital in Columbia. Numerous prominent surgeons in the city gained their initial surgical training at this institution under the mentorship of Dr. Evans.

Dr. Evans was the founder of the South Carolina Good Health Association and previously served as president of the State Negro Medical Society. At the time of her passing, she held the position of trustee at Haines Institute in Augusta, Georgia, and was an active member of the National Negro Medical Association. During World War I, Dr. Evans was appointed to the Volunteer Medical Service Corps by the National Council of Defense.

Dr. Evans never entered matrimony, but she took in multiple children who carried her surname. These individuals are John B. Evans, an insurance professional in Columbia; Mattie O. Evans, an educator at Mather

The Evans family. *From the top, beginning at the left:* John B. Evans, Artie, Myrtle Lee, Jessie Trottie Evans; *from the bottom, beginning at the right:* Dr. Matilda Evans, Dozier and Sydney Trottie Evans. *Courtesy of Smithsonian National Museum.*

Academy-Browning Home in Camden; Gresham Evans, a nursing student at Lincoln Hospital in Durham; Jessie Trottie Evans, a teacher at Waverley school; Myrtle Lee Evans from Augusta, Georgia; Edward Evans Robinson, a student at Mather Academy-Browning Home in Camden; and Sydney Trottie Evans, a student at Benedict College.

Dr. Evans paved the way for African Americans and women, serving as a beacon of inspiration as the first licensed African American medical doctor in South Carolina. Her story and legacy highlight the pursuit of happiness through fulfilling our destiny to selflessly serve humanity with our unique talents. Her memory will endure for generations to come.

# NOTES

## 1. The Ancestral Journey of Matilda Evans

1. Dickerman, "Story of a Negro Child's Resolve," 449–57.
2. Ashmead, *Historical Sketch of Chester*.
3. Cope and Ashmead, *Historic Homes and Institutions*, 459.
4. Maizlish, *Strife of Tongues*.
5. Campbell, *Slave Catchers*.
6. Landon, "Negro Migration to Canada," 22–36.
7. Larson, *Bound for the Promised Land*.
8. Northup, *Twelve Years a Slave* (Project Gutenberg eBook), 37–39.
9. Wilson, *Freedom at Risk*, 11–16.
10. Dickerman, "Story of a Negro Child's Resolve," 450.
11. "Orangeburg County," South Carolina Encyclopedia, August 16, 2022, https://www.scencyclopedia.org/sce.
12. "Orangeburg County."
13. "Orangeburg County."
14. Washington, *Story of the Negro*.
15. Dickerman, "Story of a Negro Child's Resolve," 450.
16. *Acts and Joint Resolutions of the General Assembly of the State of South Carolina*.
17. "1850 U.S. Federal Census—Slave Schedules," Ancestry, 2004, https://www.ancestry.com/.

18. "Race and Slavery Petitions," Digital Library on American Slavery, https://dlas.uncg.edu/petitions/.
19. Thompson Family Reunion Book, 1987, self-published family history book.
20. Dickerman, "Story of a Negro Child's Resolve," 449–57.
21. Dickerman, "Story of a Negro Child's Resolve," 450.
22. Dickerman, "Story of a Negro Child's Resolve," 450.
23. Dickerman, "Story of a Negro Child's Resolve," 450.
24. Dickerman, "Story of a Negro Child's Resolve," 449–57.
25. Dickerman, "Story of a Negro Child's Resolve," 451.
26. "Wills (WPA Transcripts) Charleston District 1783-1868 (L10125)," South Carolina Department of Archives and History, https://www.archivesindex.sc.gov/.
27. Brodie, *William and Ann Carter Tyler*.
28. Brodie, *William and Ann Carter Tyler*, 1.
29. Brodie, *William and Ann Carter Tyler*, 1.
30. Brodie, *William and Ann Carter Tyler*, 1.
31. Brodie, *William and Ann Carter Tyler*, 1.
32. Brodie, *William and Ann Carter Tyler*, 1.
33. Brodie, *William and Ann Carter Tyler*, 1.
34. Roof, *Kitching Genealogy*, 102.
35. Brodie, *William and Ann Carter Tyler*.
36. Brodie, *William and Ann Carter Tyler*, 1.
37. Brodie, *William and Ann Carter Tyler*, 1.
38. "U.S., Selected Federal Census Non-Population Schedules, 1850–1880," Ancestry, 2010, https://www.ancestry.com/.
39. "1860 U.S. Federal Census—Slave Schedules," Ancestry, 2010, https://www.ancestry.com/.
40. Roof, *Kitching Genealogy*, 102.
41. "U.S., Selected Federal Census Non-Population Schedules, 1850–1880."
42. "U.S., Selected Federal Census Non-Population Schedules, 1850–1880."
43. Brodie, *William and Ann Carter Tyler*.
44. Brodie, *William and Ann Carter Tyler*, 3.
45. Roof, *Kitching Genealogy*, 102.
46. *Declaration of the Immediate Causes*.
47. "Orangeburg."
48. "Orangeburg."
49. "John Wardlaw Brodie," *Charleston Daily Courier*, January 15, 1862.
50. "John Wardlaw Brodie."
51. "John Wardlaw Brodie."

52. "Wills (WPA Transcripts) Charleston District 1783–1868 (L10125)," South Carolina Department of Archives and History, https://www.archivesindex.sc.gov/.

53. "Wills (WPA Transcripts)."

54. Harvey, *Under the Heel*. This may be found in the collection of the South Carolina Historical Society.

55. Brodie, *History of the Brodie Family*, 15–16.

56. Brodie, *History of the Brodie Family*.

57. Curry, *Awakening*.

58. Curry, *Awakening*, 9.

59. Hahn et al., *Land and Labor*, 215–22.

60. Curry, *Awakening*.

61. Curry, *Awakening*, 9.

62. Brodie, *History of the Brodie Family*, 7.

63. Dickerman, "Story of a Negro Child's Resolve," 449–57.

64. Dickerman, "Story of a Negro Child's Resolve," 451.

65. "Charleston," South Carolina Encyclopedia, https://www.scencyclopedia.org/.

66. Various sources provide differing accounts regarding Dr. Evans's birth date. The date used here is derived from the *Southern Workman*, as it is the sole biography that Dr. Evans explicitly endorsed in her correspondence with Alfred Jones. Additionally, another notable year of birth is 1872, as indicated by Dr. Darlene Clark Hine in her biography, "The Corporeal and Ocular Veil: Dr. Matilda A. Evans (1872–1935) and the Complexity of Southern History," which has received validation from Dr. Evans's granddaughter Beverly Aiken-Muhammad.

67. "1870 United States Federal Census," Ancestry, https://www.ancestry.com.

68. "Founding of Aiken County," *The Intelligencer*, April 27, 1871.

69. "Founding of Aiken County."

70. "Founding of Aiken County."

71. "Founding of Aiken County."

72. "Founding of Aiken County."

73. Dickerman, "Story of a Negro Child's Resolve," 449–57.

74. Smyrna Missionary Baptist Church Anniversary Book.

75. Smyrna Missionary Baptist Church Anniversary Book.

76. Smyrna Missionary Baptist Church Anniversary Book.

77. Smyrna Missionary Baptist Church Anniversary Book.

78. Smyrna Missionary Baptist Church Anniversary Book.

79. Smyrna Missionary Baptist Church Anniversary Book.

80. Smyrna Missionary Baptist Church Anniversary Book.
81. Artee Quattlebaum Brown, granddaughter of Isaac and Charlotte Thompson-Quattlebaum, in person conversation on June 15, 2008, with Walter B. Curry Jr. at Artee's home in Salley, South Carolina.
82. Brown, conversation.
83. Curry, *Thompson Family*.
84. Curry, *Awakening*, 108–9.
85. Curry, *Awakening*, 108–9.
86. "Ellenton Riot," *Newberry Weekly Herald*, October 4, 1876.
87. Brown, conversation.
88. Dickerman, "Story of a Negro Child's Resolve," 449–57.
89. Dickerman, "Story of a Negro Child's Resolve," 449–57.
90. "1880 United States Federal Census," Ancestry, https://www.ancestry.com.
91. *Times and Democrat*, June 18, 1890.
92. *Times and Democrat*, June 18, 1890.
93. *Times and Democrat*, June 18, 1890.
94. 1880 United States Federal Census."
95. Dickerman, "Story of a Negro Child's Resolve," 449–57.
96. Dickerman, "Story of a Negro Child's Resolve," 449–57.
97. Dickerman, "Story of a Negro Child's Resolve," 449–57.
98. Dickerman, "Story of a Negro Child's Resolve," 449–57.
99. "John Corley—Dr. Matilda Evans," *Aiken Standard*, November 8, 1899.
100. Dickerman, "Story of a Negro Child's Resolve," 449–57.

## 2. Matilda Evans's Educational Journey

101. Price, "School Segregation," 121–37.
102. Price, "School Segregation," 122.
103. Price, "School Segregation," 123.
104. Price, "School Segregation," 125.
105. Price, "School Segregation," 125.
106. Price, "School Segregation," 125.
107. "Stono Rebellion," *The State*, February 3, 2000.
108. "Slave Codes," South Carolina Encyclopedia, https://www.sccncyclopcdia.org.
109. "Slave Codes."
110. Birnie, "Education of the Negro," 13–21.

111. "The 'Mudsill' Theory by James Henry Hammond," *Africans in America*, 2019, https://www.pbs.org.
112. Cornelius, "'We Slipped and Learned to Read,'" 171–86.
113. "Narrative of the Life of Frederick Douglass," Pressbooks, https://pressbooks.howardcc.edu.
114. Woodson, *Mis-Education of the Negro*, 25.
115. "Quakers—South Carolina Encyclopedia." South Carolina Encyclopedia, June 20, 2016, https://www.scencyclopedia.org.
116. "Quakers."
117. "Quakers."
118. "Quakers."
119. Martha Schofield Papers, SFHL-RG5-134, Friends Historical Library of Swarthmore College, A00181091.
120. Martha Schofield Papers, SFHL-RG5-134.
121. Martha Schofield Papers, SFHL-RG5-134, 14.
122. Martha Schofield Papers, SFHL-RG5-134, 14.
123. Martha Schofield Papers, SFHL-RG5-134, 28.
124. Martha Schofield Papers, SFHL-RG5-134, 29.
125. Reverend Price served as pastor of Sardis Missionary Baptist Church in the 1870s.
126. Martha Schofield Papers, SFHL-RG5-134.
127. Dickerman, "Story of a Negro Child's Resolve," 449–57.
128. Dickerman, "Story of a Negro Child's Resolve," 452.
129. Dickerman, "Story of a Negro Child's Resolve," 453.
130. Dickerman, "Story of a Negro Child's Resolve," 453.
131. Dickerman, "Story of a Negro Child's Resolve," 453.
132. Ghosh, "Historical Analysis of Health Institutions."
133. Ghosh, "Historical Analysis of Health Institutions."
134. Ghosh, "Historical Analysis of Health Institutions."
135. Woodson, *Mis-Education of the Negro*, 75.
136. Ghosh, "Historical Analysis of Health Institutions."
137. Washington, *Up from Slavery*, 30.
138. Washington, *Up from Slavery*, 127.
139. Washington, *Up from Slavery*, 128.
140. Du Bois, *Souls of Black Folk*, 43, 44.
141. "Woman's Medical College of Pennsylvania," Encyclopedia of Greater Philadelphia, https://philadelphiaencyclopedia.org.
142. Dixon, *Hidden History of Chester County*.
143. "Woman's Medical College of Pennsylvania."

144. "Woman's Medical College of Pennsylvania."
145. "Woman's Medical College of Pennsylvania."
146. *Fentonville Observer*, August 11, 1854.
147. "The First Female Medical College: 'Will You Accept or Reject Them?', Doctor or Doctress? https://doctordoctress.org.
148. "First Female Medical College."
149. Lindhost, "Sarah Mapps Douglass."
150. "Letter from Matilda Evans to Alfred Jones March 13, 1907, Correspondence," Doctor or Doctress? https://doctordoctress.org.
151. "Letter from Matilda Evans to Alfred Jones."
152. "M.A. Evans," *Aiken Standard*, June 2, 1897.

## 3. Matilda Evans Receives Her Medical License in South Carolina

153. Vennie Deas-Moore, "Traditional Medicine," South Carolina Encyclopedia, June 28, 2016, https://www.scencyclopedia.org/sce/.
154. Deas-Moore, "Traditional Medicine."
155. Deas-Moore, "Traditional Medicine."
156. Hamowy, "Early Development of Medical Licensing Laws."
157. "State Board of Medical Examiners," *Times and Democrat*, January 17, 1894.
158. "State Board of Medical Examiners."
159. "Colored Woman Physician," *County Record*, December 9, 1897.
160. Original copy of Dr. Matilda Evans's license.

## 4. Matilda Evans: The Woman Who Made a Significant Impact on Both Her Race and the State of South Carolina

161. Dickerman, "Story of a Negro Child's Resolve," 449–57.
162. Dickerman, "Story of a Negro Child's Resolve," 449–57.
163. Dickerman, "Story of a Negro Child's Resolve," 449–57.
164. Matilda A. Evans Collection, 1897–1977, South Caroliniana Library, 1897.
165. "Flames Destroy Negro Hospital," *Bamberg Herald*, May 11, 1911.
166. "Matilda A. Evans, Taylor Lane Hospital and Training School For Nurses," *The State*, May 13, 1905.
167. Dickerman, "Story of a Negro Child's Resolve," 449–57.
168. Dickerman, "Story of a Negro Child's Resolve," 449–57.
169. Evans, *Brief History of the Evans Clinic*.

170. "Used Hatchet on Negro's Head," *Bamberg Herald*, October 6, 1910.
171. "Struck by a Train, Negro Run Over Last Night in the Union Depot Yard, *The State*, January 28, 1905.
172. "Died from Her Burns, Negro Woman Died After Three Weeks' Suffering," *The State*, August 16, 1904.
173. "Small 'Live' Bone Operation at Taylor Lane Hospital," *Columbia Record*, July 8, 1910.
174. "Bitten by a Rattlesnake," *The State*, August 7, 1906.
175. "Matilda A Evans, Pratt Nurse Training School, Benedict College," *The State*, January 21, 1902.
176. Ghosh, "Historical Analysis of Health Institutions."
177. Ghosh, "Historical Analysis of Health Institutions," 33.
178. Dickerman, "Story of a Negro Child's Resolve," 449–57.
179. Dickerman, "Story of a Negro Child's Resolve," 449–57.
180. Roberts, *True Likeness*.
181. Matilda A. Evans Collection, 1897–1977.
182. Matilda A. Evans Collection, 1897–1977.
183. Matilda A. Evans Collection, 1897–1977.
184. "Matilda A. Evans, H. Van Buren, Taylor Lane Hospital," *The State*, January 23, 1909.
185. "Matilda A. Evans, H. Van Buren."
186. "Matilda A. Evans, H. Van Buren."
187. "For Taylor Lane Colored Hospital, Mass Meeting at Allen University for Purpose of Doing Something," *Columbia Record*, April 11, 1911.
188. "For Taylor Lane Colored Hospital."
189. "For Taylor Lane Colored Hospital."
190. "Flames Destroy Negro Hospital."
191. "Matilda Evans Story," *The State*, January 10, 1910.
192. "Matilda A. Evans, Kidney Complaint, Taylor Lane Hospital," *Southern Indicator*, July 25, 1914.
193. "Declaration and Petition for Incorporation for Negro Health Association—Dr. Matilda Evans," *Columbia Record*, July 8, 1916.
194. "Declaration and Petition for Incorporation."
195. "Negro Association of South Carolina, Saint Luke Hospital," *Columbia Record*, October 22, 1916.
196. Evans, "Cheap Living, Poverty, Disease and Death."
197. Evans, "Cheap Living, Poverty, Disease and Death."
198. "Negro Health Association of South Carolina Offers St. Luke's to Government," *Sunday Record*, September 1, 1918.

199. Evans, "Cheap Living, Poverty, Disease and Death."
200. "Negro Red Cross Branch Is Active—Dr. Matilda Evans," *Columbia Record*, July 4, 1917.
201. "Dr. Matilda Evans, Influenza Brings Distress to Many," *The State*, October 13, 1918.
202. "Dr. Matida Evans, Negro Red Cross Call, Should Give Aid in Nursing Sick," *The State*, October 12, 1918.
203. "Newborn Baby Left on Steps—Dr. Matilda Evans," *Columbia Record*, May 25, 1923.
204. Evans, *Brief History of the Evans Clinic*.
205. "Negro Children's Clinic Reaches Many Patients," *The State*, September 17, 1930.
206. "The Columbia Clinic Preparing to Meet All Demands," *Palmetto Leader*, October 18, 1930.
207. Evans, *Brief History of the Evans Clinic*.
208. Evans, *Brief History of the Evans Clinic*.
209. Columbia Clinic Preparing to Meet All Demands.".
210. "Negro Children's Clinic Reaches Many."
211. "Surprise Party and Banquet at Columbia Clinic," *Palmetto Leader*, December 6, 1930.
212. Evans, *Brief History of the Evans Clinic*.
213. Evans, *Brief History of the Evans Clinic*.
214. Evans, *Brief History of the Evans Clinic*.
215. "Budget for City for 1935 as Set by City Council," *The State*, March 7, 1935.
216. "Evans Clinic to Hold Mass Meeting Sunday," *Columbia Record*, May 9, 1933.
217. "Evans Clinic to Hold Mass Meeting Sunday."
218. "Whilden Pleads Again in Aid Evans Clinic," *The State*, June 27, 1933.
219. "Must Raise Two Thousand Dollars for Maintenance of Evans Clinic," *The State*, August 15, 1933.
220. "The Matilda Evans Clinic," *The State*, November 15, 1933.
221. "Negro Children Are Remembered," *The State*, December 27, 1933.
222. "Negro Children Are Given Dinner," *The State*, December 1, 1933.
223. "Negro Children Are Remembered."

## 5. Matilda Evans: Her Roles as a Civic Advocate and Entrepreneur

224. Clifford Kuhn and Gregory Mixon, "Atlanta Race Massacre of 1906," *New Georgia Encyclopedia*, November 14, 2022, https://www. georgiaencyclopedia.org/.
225. Kuhn and Mixon, "Atlanta Race Massacre."
226. Kuhn and Mixon, "Atlanta Race Massacre."
227. Kuhn and Mixon, "Atlanta Race Massacre."
228. Kuhn and Mixon, "Atlanta Race Massacre."
229. Kuhn and Mixon, "Atlanta Race Massacre."
230. Kuhn and Mixon, "Atlanta Race Massacre."
231. Kuhn and Mixon, "Atlanta Race Massacre."
232. Evans, *Martha Schofield*, accessible via Project Gutenberg, https://www. gutenberg.org/.
233. Evans, *Martha Schofield*.
234. "Carroll, Richard." South Carolina Encyclopedia, July 30, 2024, https://www.scencyclopedia.org.
235. "Carroll, Richard."
236. "Carroll, Richard."
237. "Carroll, Richard."
238. "Carroll, Richard."
239. "Carroll, Richard."
240. "Matilda A. Evans, Race Conference to Begin Today, Community Service," *The State*, January 23, 1907.
241. "Matilda A. Evans, Race Conference."
242. "Matilda A. Evans, Race Conference."
243. Jackson, "Booker T. Washington," 192–220.
244. Washington, *Story of the Negro*.
245. "Get the Habit," *Southern Indicator*, August 12, 1922.
246. "Get the Habit."
247. "Farmers' Picnic & Barbecue," *Southern Indicator*, August 12, 1922.
248. "Negro Fair Body Elects Executives," *The State*, October 29, 1925.
249. "Negro Fair."
250. "Negro Fair Is Ready to Open," *Columbia Record*, October 26, 1925.
251. "Negroes Conclude Annual Convention," *The State*, June 23, 1924.
252. "Negroes Conclude Annual Convention."
253. "To Meet Tonight at Zion Baptist, Negroes Plan for Sunday School Conference," *The State*, June 8, 1926.
254. "To Meet Tonight at Zion Baptist."

255. "Negro Delegates Are Pouring In, Attendance Upon Sunday School Congress Expected to Reach Thousands," *Columbia Record*, June 9, 1926.
256. "Negro Delegates Are Pouring In."
257. "Negro Delegates Are Pouring In."
258. "Negro Delegates Are Pouring In."
259. Evans, *Martha Schofield*.
260. Evans, *Martha Schofield*.
261. Jackson, "Booker T. Washington," 192–220.
262. "State League Meets, Negro Business Mean Hold Conference Here," *The State*, July 18, 1920.
263. "State League Meets."
264. "The Mutual Relief & Benevolent Association," *Columbia Record*, October 22, 1916.
265. "Mutual Relief & Benevolent Association."
266. "Black South Carolinians in World War I," South Carolina Public Radio, https://www.southcarolinapublicradio.org/.
267. "The Official Roster of South Carolina Soldiers, Sailors and Marines in the World War, 1917–18," South Carolina State Library Digital Collections, https://dc.statelibrary.sc.gov/home.
268. Megginson, "Black South Carolinians in World War I," 153–73.
269. "Negroes Will Try to Raise $100,000," *The State*, January 24, 1919.
270. "Negroes Will Try to Raise $100,000."
271. "Will Devise Plans to Protect Negro Women—Dr. Matilda Evans," *Columbia Record*, July 4, 1917.
272. "Will Devise Plans to Protect Negro Women."
273. "Negroes Tender Their Services," *The State*, April 5, 1917.
274. "Negroes Tender Their Services."
275. "Negroes Tender Their Services."
276. "Negroes Tender Their Services."
277. "Negroes Tender Their Services."
278. "Negroes Tender Their Services."
279. "Negroes Tender Their Services."
280. "Negroes Tender Their Services."
281. Dickerman, "Story of a Negro Child's Resolve," 449–57.
282. "The Evesco Products," *Sunday Record*, November 9, 1930.
283. "Evesco Products."

## 6. Matilda Evans: In Her Last Days

284. "Matilda Evans Tendered Banquet," *The State*, March 3, 1935.
285. "Matilda Evans Tendered Banquet."
286. "Dr. Matilda Evans Obituary," *The State*, November 18, 1935.
287. "Dr. Matilda Evans Obituary."
288. "Matilda A. Evans, Colored Folk Hold Meetings, Community Service," *Columbia Record*, January 12, 1910.

# BIBLIOGRAPHY

*Acts and Joint Resolutions of the General Assembly of the State of South Carolina.* United States: Creative Media Partners, LLC, 2019.

Ashmead, Henry Graham. *Historical Sketch of Chester, on Delaware.* Republican Steam Printing House, 1883.

Birnie, C.W. "Education of the Negro in Charleston, South Carolina, prior to the Civil War." *Journal of Negro History* 12, no. 1 (1927): 13–21.

Brodie, A.L. *A History of the Brodie Family 1754–1983.* Self-published, 1994.

———. *William and Ann Carter Tyler and Some of Their Descendants 1604–2008.* Self-published, 2009.

Campbell, Stanley W. *The Slave Catchers: Enforcement of the Fugitive Slave Law, 1850–1860.* University of North Carolina Press, 1970.

Cope, Gilbert, and Henry Graham Ashmead. *Historic Homes and Institutions and Genealogical and Personal Memoirs of Chester and Delaware Counties, Pennsylvania.* Vol. 2. Lewis Publishing Company, 1904.

Cornelius, Janet. "'We Slipped and Learned to Read:' Slave Accounts of the Literacy Process, 1830–1865." *Phylon* 44, no. 3 (1983): 171–86.

Curry, Walter. *The Awakening: The Seawright-Ellison Family Saga*, vol.1, *A Narrative History*. Palmetto Publishing, 2021.

———. *The Thompson Family: Untold Stories From The Past (1830–1960)*. Amazon KDP Services, 2019.

*Declaration of the Immediate Causes Which Induce and Justify the Secession of South Carolina from the Federal Union*. Constitutional Convention (1860–1862). S 131055. South Carolina Department of Archives and History, Columbia, South Carolina, December 24, 1860.

Dickerman, G.S. "The Story of a Negro Child's Resolve." In *The Southern Workman*. Hampton Institute Press, 1906.

Dixon, Mark. *The Hidden History of Chester County: Lost Tales from the Delaware and Brandywine Valleys*. The History Press, 2011.

Du Bois, W.E.B. *The Souls of Black Folk*. Barnes & Noble Books, 2003.

Evans, Matilda. *A Brief History of the Evans Clinic: 1235 Harden Street*. Columbia, SC, 1932.

———. "Cheap Living, Poverty, Disease and Death Lay Heavy Annual Tax on People Everywhere." *Negro Health Journal*, September 1916.

———. *Martha Schofield, Pioneer Negro Educator: Historical and Philosophical Review of Reconstruction Period of South Carolina*. DuPre Printing Company, 1916.

Ghosh, Anusha. "A Historical Analysis of Health Institutions, Professionals, and Advocates in the Civil Rights Movement in Columbia, South Carolina." Thesis, South Carolina Honors College, 2024.

Hahn, Steven, Steven F. Millier, Susan E. O'Donovan, John C. Rodrigue and Leslie S. Rowland, eds. *Land and Labor*, series 3, volume 1. University of North Carolina Press, 2008.

Hamowy, Ronald. "The Early Development of Medical Licensing Laws in the United States, 1875–1900." *Journal of Libertarian Studies* 3, no. 1 (1979): 73–119.

Harvey, Mary Phillips. *Under the Heel of the Invader*. Self-published circa 1925.

Jackson, David H. "Booker T. Washington in South Carolina, March 1909." *South Carolina Historical Magazine* 113, no. 3 (2012): 192–220.

Landon, Fred "The Negro Migration to Canada After the Passing of the Fugitive Slave Act." *Journal of Negro History* 5, no. 1 (1920): 22–36.

Larson, Kate Clifford. *Bound for the Promised Land: Harriet Tubman, Portrait of an American Hero*. Ballantine, 2004.

Lindhost, Marie. "Sarah Mapps Douglass: The Emergence of an African American Educator/Activist in 19th Century Philadelphia." PhD diss., Pennsylvania State University, 1995.

Maizlish, Stephen E. *A Strife of Tongues: The Compromise of 1850 and the Ideological Foundations of the American Civil War*. University of Virginia Press, 2018.

Megginson, W.J. "Black South Carolinians in World War I: The 'Official Roster' as a Resource for Local History, Mobility, and African-American History." *South Carolina Historical Magazine* 96, no. 2 (1995): 153–73.

Northup, Solomon. *Twelve Years a Slave: Narrative of Solomon Northup, a Citizen of New-York, Kidnapped in Washington City in 1841, and Rescued in 1853, from a Cotton Plantation near the Red River in Louisiana*. Project Gutenberg eBook. https://www.gutenberg.org..

Price, Edward J. "School Segregation in Nineteenth-Century Pennsylvania." *Pennsylvania History* 43, no. 2 (1976): 121–37.

Roberts, Richard Samuel. *A True Likeness: The Black South of Richard Samuel Roberts, 1920–1936*. Edited by Thomas L. Johnson and Phillip C. Dunn. Bruccoli Clark & Algonquin Books of Chapel Hill, n.d.

Roof, Micheal Kitching. *Kitching Genealogy: Matthew Kitching, Wife, and Descendants of South Carolina, 1806–Present*. Self-published, 2009.Washington, Booker T. *The Story of the Negro: The Rise of the Race from Slavery*, 1909.

———. *Up from Slavery*. Barnes & Noble, 1901.

Wilson, Carol. *Freedom at Risk: The Kidnapping of Free Blacks in America, 1780–1865*. University Press of Kentucky, 1994.

Woodson, Carter G. *The Mis-Education of the Negro*. Emworld Inc., 1933.

# ABOUT THE AUTHORS

DR. WALTER B. CURRY JR. hails from Orangeburg, South Carolina. He obtained a bachelor's degree in political science from South Carolina State University and furthered his education with graduate degrees, culminating in a doctorate in curriculum and instruction from Argosy University in Sarasota. In 2018, he established Renaissance Publications LLC, a self-publishing venture dedicated to producing works that highlight African American history through the lens of ancestry. Dr. Curry is the author of two award-winning books: *The Thompson Family: Untold Stories from the Past (1830–1960)* and *The Awakening: The Seawright-Ellison Family Saga*, vol. 1, *A Narrative History*, both of which explore his family's history from slavery through significant historical periods. He is the lead Research Consultant to The Dr. Matilda A. Evans Educational Foundation, LLC. He has actively participated in book signings and presentations at various local and national venues, including conferences, workshops, bookstores and schools.

Dr. Walter B. Curry Jr.

BEVERLY AIKEN-MUHAMMAD is the eldest granddaughter of Dr. Matilda A. Evans, and the oldest daughter of Mattie Evans Aiken. She was born in Camden, South Carolina, and grew up in both Camden and Columbia.

She is the Founder, Executive Director and CEO of The Dr. Matilda A. Evans Educational Foundation LLC, a recognized 501(c)(3) non-profit organization. Her educational background includes attending Mather Academy in Camden and Benedict College in Columbia, as well as Montclair Teachers College in New Jersey and the University of The District of Columbia in Washington, D.C. She is a published author of several books and articles. She has also held the position of Press Secretary for a congressional campaign, a United States Senate campaign and a State Board of Education campaign. She has contributed as an editorial writer for *The*

Beverly Aiken-Muhammad.

*Washington Afro American*, *Capitol Spotlight* and *News Dimensions* newspapers. She is a retired teacher and has also worked in hospital administration. For over forty-three years, she has been married to Timothy Muhammad, with whom she has three children: Kariem Hammonds, Akbar Ali and Nadia J. Muhammad, who was formerly Ms. Benedict College 2006–07.

ANUSHA GHOSH is currently pursuing her MD at the University of South Carolina–Columbia, having earned her Bachelor of Science degree from the University of South Carolina Honors College with a focus on public health, language and history. She is dedicated to enhancing the healthcare system, especially for marginalized and stigmatized populations. Her passion for utilizing local public history as a means of preserving cultural heritage and informing contemporary public health efforts was ignited after her initial medical history course. Originally

Anusha Ghosh.

from Greenville, South Carolina, she is the eldest daughter of Bengali Indian immigrants Soma and Kripan Ghosh and has two younger siblings, Ayush and Ava. In addition to her academic pursuits, Anusha actively volunteers with local nonprofits, enjoys reading fiction and appreciates taking scenic walks.